MOTHERHOOD OR CAREER?

"When you are asked, as you are so often, if you are going to work or get married (meaning be a mother, too), it's hard to answer because *you are being asked the wrong question*. The right question for women is how can we plan all of our crucial life-giving tasks in school, with family and friends, at work and play, so that they are fully integrated?"

—Joyce Slayton Mitchell,
From the Introduction

The simple truth today is that you don't have to sacrifice a money-making job in order to be a mother. You can develop career skills *while* you raise your child, because the skills and personal growth that come from being a mother are practical assets you can use to advance yourself in a career.

BE A MOTHER AND MORE shows you how to make career decisions once you've decided to be a mother. How to plan financially for your child's needs, how to put your talents to work in the job market, how to become the complete, fulfilled woman you want to be.

"Meets a growing need for young women whose desire for career and life planning has been largely ignored or discounted."

—Lucia H. Bequaert,
Executive Director, Boston YWCA

BE A MOTHER ... AND MORE

CAREER AND LIFE PLANNING

by Joyce Slayton Mitchell

BANTAM BOOKS
TORONTO · NEW YORK · LONDON

BE A MOTHER AND MORE
A Bantam Book/November 1980

Acknowledgments
*"Growing Children Need Growing Parents" by Helen DeRosis,
M.D. from* Parent Power: Child Power, *New York: Bobbs-Merrill.
Copyright © 1974 by the author. Excerpts from* Where Are We
Running *copyright © 1979 and* Journal of a Happy Woman
*copyright © 1973 by June Strong. "Are You A Gal Who
Needs to Get Pregnant?" copyright © 1980 by Lise Brackett.
"Love Is More Than a Feeling," copyright © 1980 by
Reverend Patricia Budd Kepler. "A Half-Day with 8-Month-Old
Kate," copyright © 1980 by Larry Daloz. "Human Rights
Are the Rights of Children," copyright © 1980 by
Virginia Coigney. "Life Career Skills," copyright © 1980
by Ellen J. Wallach.*

ISBN 0-553-13926-6

Published simultaneously in the United States and Canada

---

*Bantam Books are published by Bantam Books, Inc. Its trade-
mark, consisting of the words "Bantam Books" and the por-
trayal of a bantam, is Registered in U.S. Patent and Trademark
Office and in other countries. Marca Registrada. Bantam
Books, Inc., 666 Fifth Avenue, New York, New York 10103.*

PRINTED IN THE UNITED STATES OF AMERICA

0 9 8 7 6 5 4 3 2 1

TO MARGARET MEAD

Who loved being a mother . . .
and who loved being more

CONTRIBUTORS

Virginia Coigney, Director,
Patient and Community Relations,
Danbury Hospital, Danbury, Connecticut.

Lary Daloz, Director,
Learning Systems Design, Glover, Vermont.

Helen A. DeRosis, Associate Clinical Professor
in Psychiatry, New York University School
of Medicine, New York, New York.

Patricia Budd Kepler, Director,
Ministerial Studies, Harvard Divinity
School, Cambridge, Massachusetts.

Ellen J. Wallach, Career Development Consultant,
Lexington, Massachusetts.

CONTENTS

BE A MOTHER

. . . AND MORE

It is a pleasure to thank the parents, mothers-to-be, interested women, teenagers, the contributors, and my editor who shaped the directions of this book.

I am especially grateful to the pregnant teenagers from the Elizabeth Lund Home and the young mothers who have infants in the Visiting Nurses Association Daycare Center who added life to this book by describing their personal experiences.

Also to Helen King, associate director and casework supervisor, and Alice Hobart, public relations director of the Elizabeth Lund Home, a residential care center for unmarried mothers in Burlington, Vermont.

And to Elizabeth J. Davis, director of the Visiting Nurses Association, and Jeanne Simon, director of the VNA Daycare Center, Burlington, Vermont, who arranged interviews and shared experiences with employed mothers.

Thanks, too, to Maggie Maurice, lifestyles editor of *The Burlington Free Press* (Vermont), who shared her materials and contacts for two-career families.

I owe my appreciation to June Strong for giving her permission to quote from her book, *Journal of a Happy Woman,* Southern Publishing Association.

Sylvia Porter's Money Book (Avon Books) was a basic source of information, especially for the chapter, "Money: Making and Managing It."

Lise Brackett gave her permission to adapt her creative cartoon-style booklet, *Are You a Gal/ Guy Who Needs to get Pregnant?* Send 75¢ for the original to: RFD #3, Toad Hollow Press, Montpelier, Vermont 05602

I owe a special thanks to my editor, Toni Burbank, who loved the "mother book" from the beginning. As a new mother and a very creative editor, Toni added much discernment to the book.

Our teenagers, Ned and Elizabeth have my thanks with love for shaping up the "Shape Up or Watch Out Test," which resulted in an expanded version of the test and an unsolicited insight into our family's discipline situation!

JSM
Wolcott, Vermont

A BABY, MAYBE?

Most of us take it for granted that we will grow up, get married, and live happily ever after. Most of us take it for granted that we will have a family. When you are a young woman there is a lot of hope in your life, as there should be. But something seems to go wrong for many older women, for those who have had their babies, and are in troubled relationships with their husbands—the father of their babies.

How can you prevent your hope from dying, as you sometimes observe the despair in the lives of your relatives, neighbors and friends? What can you do now that will turn your hope for a lovely family into a reality? Questioning the things often taken for granted can help. For example, asking yourself whether you should have a baby or not can lead to these questions: If I have a baby, when should I have it? If I get married and if I enjoy sex because I'm a sexual being, does a baby have to automatically follow? If I have a baby, what are the other options in my life? "A baby, maybe?" is a question that can turn things around for you so that living happily ever after is not accidental, it's by *your* design, your plan.

BE A MOTHER
... AND MORE:
CAREER AND
LIFE PLANNING

It's hard to plan your life. Everyone acts as though you should keep thinking about and deciding what you are going to be, even though you know that you'll probably get married and be a mother. In school, teachers and counselors ask about your intended career as if you were going to start a career and keep it up, just as your brothers and boyfriends do. Most people assume that you're going to be a mother, but nobody talks about what that has to do with anything else—such as a job or a career or graduate school or old age. The world seems to package a woman's life and work in unreal but neatly wrapped boxes. One box is a mother at home with her children, and another completely separate box is way over there somewhere and it's called work. Meaning paid work, of course. And then there are the other parts of your life which are packaged as education or hobbies or sports.

When you are asked, as you are so often, if you are going to work or get married (meaning be a mother too) it's hard to answer because *you are being asked the wrong question*. The right question for women is how can we plan all of our crucial life-giving tasks in school, with family and friends, at work and play, so

3

that they are fully integrated together? In other words, how can we get our packaging together?

If you find yourself confused, ask yourself these questions: How do school and family, and work take my time and energy? How do these tasks give me energy? How will these parts of my life change? What does family have to do with friends?

WHAT DOES MOTHERHOOD HAVE TO DO WITH WORK?

It used to be that most mothers of school-age children were not employed outside their homes. Today things are different. Everyone, especially young women, should know that more than 1 in every 3 mothers in the United States with *pre-school* children (41 percent) is employed outside her home. That's children under six years old. And "employed" means fulltime employment. The rate is even higher for mothers with school-age children under 18 where more than one in every 2 mothers (58 percent) is employed.

Why are all these mothers working? Because, just like men, they need the money. They need the money to support themselves and their children. Often, when you hear that 58 percent of the mothers in America are employed fulltime, you assume that 100 percent of the men are employed in our country. It may be helpful for you to know that only 75 percent of the eligible men from 16 to 65 years old are fulltime workers. When you realize that 58 percent of the mothers, and 75 percent of the eligible men work fulltime, it doesn't appear to be such a great difference. And with that little difference, it is obvious that career planning should be as serious a business for young women as it is for young men.

You may have career planning or career education in your school or college. Or you may have educators talking to you about your career. What exactly is a career? What does "career" mean? How does a man's career differ from a woman's career?

It doesn't! A career means all the work, *paid or unpaid, fulltime* or *parttime,* that a person does in a lifetime. In other words, right now your school work is a part of your career. Your parttime work and summer work (volunteer or paid) are part of your career. A career starts in early childhood education and extends through retirement. There isn't any work you do that doesn't count as part of your career. Caring for babies and children, managing a home, working at fund-raising, and working as an engineer, or parttime in sales, are all within your career development. It's all work, even though some is paid and some unpaid, some parttime or fulltime or overtime. Work requires skills, to be learned and managed. A skill is a developed aptitude or ability relating to a specific job or occupation. Many skills are transferable from one job to the next within your overall career. Some transferable skills that you may learn at work (including work at home) are speaking, listening, letter writing, leadership, decision making, persuasion, time management.

What does motherhood have to do with work? Motherhood *is* work. Work where we learn and develop skills. Work where most women spend many years of their total career. And that work counts in our career development as definitely as work in the military counts, or work in apprenticeship, or college, or the first five years on a paid job.

WHAT DOES A MOTHER DO IN THE FAMILY?

The family is changing. You hear it everywhere. Magazines, newspapers, the Department of Labor and the Bureau of the Census are all reporting it. But they say that many of us are still thinking that a father earns the money, while a mother stays at home tending the house and kids. In 1978, however, this Dick and Jane version of the family was true of only 7 percent of all American families! Almost as many families (6.2 percent) are headed by women alone, with one or more children at home. Sometimes men are single parents too, but not often, only about half of one percent (0.6 percent) of single-parent families are headed by men. The largest group of married couples with children (18.5 percent) are the families where both the mother and the father are fulltime wage-earners with one or more children at home.

What do mothers do? Most of them make money—in addition to the other mother things.

From these statistics we can see clearly one thing about the family that is *not* changing. Young women are still having babies and taking care of them. The family structure—with whom and where you live and who pays for it—may be changing, but the fact that young women are still primarily responsible for child-care (or for finding someone else to do it) is not changing. The big change is that mothers of all ages are helping to support their children financially.

The more the responsibilities in the family change, the clearer our place is going to be in the changing family. As a young woman in the midst of the changing expectations for mothers in childcare *and* making money, you have a number of questions to think through: Where am I? What are my choices? Where can I go with my career? When is the best time for *me* to have a baby? If and when I have a baby, who is going to be financially and emotionally responsible for it? Who can show me what it's like? Where do I learn?

THE MOTHER IMAGE

"I stand for Motherhood, America, a hot lunch for orphans . . ." sings Carol Channing in *Hello, Dolly!* You have all heard about the typical American-as-apple-pie mother: She loves her children all of the time, she has boundless energy to nurture and comfort them, she is always calm and even-tempered, she looks fantastically fresh and young, she is happiest when she is serving her children peanut-butter sandwiches, or driving them to their lessons, or cleaning their dirty little clothes until they are whiter than white. Television, Hollywood, popular songs, and Mother's Day are all clear about this image of the perfect mother. Runaway boys and sailors even wear her tattooed in a heart on their arm—kind of like a saint or a Madonna.

At the other extreme of this dream-world image of

mother is the protesting-type mother who is rebeling from this "never to be achieved" perfect image.

The protesting mothers have written a lot of books. If you notice the titles of the books, you'll catch on to some of the attitudes about being a mother from women who have tried to be perfect for a few years and been frustrated by their feelings of failure and guilt. *The Mother Knot, Mother's Day Is over, Juggling: The Art of Balancing Marriage, Motherhood and a Career, The Baby Trap, Of Woman Born*—these mother books describe the traps or predicaments that young mothers get themselves into, and are trying to work themselves out of. They are asking: If motherhood is as rewarding and fulfilling as we were brought up to believe, why aren't men fighting for the privilege? Why isn't it easier to share the fulfilling task with others?

There are other mother books. *The Welfare Mother, Report from the Heart, Mothers and Daughters, The Future of Motherhood, My Mother Myself, The Journey of a Happy Woman* and *Motherlove*. These books describe poor women, mothers with nine children and four husbands, mothers who adore their new-born infants but have to go off to work and leave them with the woman downstairs who doesn't adore the baby, mothers who tie a key around their first-grader's neck so the young student can open the door to the empty house after school before she gets home exhausted at six, mothers who spend the day on the factory line or in the typing pool and dream of being at home with their 3- and 5-year-olds, and meeting their 6-year-old after school. Some of these mother's books tell about the wonder of walking with a child through the woods, of taking their 3-year-olds by the hand to cross a busy street, and the complete joy of being with children and learning the marvels of what is natural all over again through the eyes of the young.

There is a tremendous difference between the Hollywood, television, and advertising model of the ideal mother, and the real-life mothers who feel trapped, ripped off, and tied down, often without the money to hire someone to care for the baby or buy the kind of food they want to provide. Most mothers are not at one extreme or the other, although the odds are stacked against very young mothers who have unplanned babies. The planned baby can be systematically provided for, but the unplanned baby is often a terrible shock.

Mothers who feel they can never measure up to what the ideal is have unreal expectations for themselves. After hearing so much about "the perfect mother," young women often feel that they shouldn't even get angry with their children; that instead, they should meet all the needs of their children plus their husband plus their boss at work, plus their own parents, plus their husband's parents; that they should be with their children all of the time and consider themselves lucky to have the opportunity. The result is that G-U-I-L-T spells mother.

How do young women end up to be one kind of a mother or another? Think about the following aspects of motherhood.

LEARNING THE MOTHER ROLE

One way to learn what you will be like as a mother—before you become one—is to look at your own family, your mother, your aunts, your cousins. Describe your mother. Notice how everyone relates to your mom. Think about the kind of role that you as a daughter have with your mother, the kind of role she has with *her* mother. What expectations do you have of your mother *because* she is your mother? How about the males in the family, your brothers and your father? What do they expect of her? Do you want to be like your mom? In what ways do you want to be different? What were her choices when she was your age? Are they different from your choices? What was expected of her then? What is expected of you now? Try these questions with your friends' mothers, and your mother's friends.

With some effort and observation on your part, you can pull away from the media image of perfect motherhood and from the other extreme of a mother who is trapped by the traditional mother role. You can think through your own choices. The part of the country where you grow up, your ethnic background, your age, your education and the education and color of your family all make a difference in your choices and the expectations others have of you.

Another way to learn in advance about what it's like to be a mother is to read about mothers—to read about as many different types and life-styles as you can.

You can also learn by talking to young mothers and asking them what it's like. Ask them what it's like compared to what they thought it would be like? What do they regret not knowing more about before they had their babies; about themselves, about motherhood, about babies, about work, about money? About getting along with fathers? You will probably learn most from young women like yourself, but you may get some ideas about being a mother from people who aren't like you, who come from a different educational, economic or racial background.

A MILLION WAYS TO BE A MOM

It's just not true that there are only certain conditions that make it OK to be a mother. It's not true that you have to be married, to be over 18 (or under 30), to be like your mother, to be supported by a husband, to love all little children, to be mature, to be loving and giving *all the time*, in order to be a successful mother. You can be a welfare mother, a lesbian mother, a black mother, a dropout mother, a mother alone—or with a husband, or a friend, or family—a single mother, a disabled mother. All of these are ways for some women to be a mom.

And it's OK. It really is. Whatever your situation, you can turn the things that don't work around. You can build on the good things you've got going in order to work things out in a way that makes it OK for *you* to be a mom. Remember: A mother is not *all* you are. You also may be a wife, friend, partner, wage-earner, sister, daughter.

Some successful mothers have a partner to help with the parenting of their children: and some don't. Some mothers have parents, or friends, or an agency to help. And some mothers don't. But no matter who or how many you have for help, you yourself are still primarily responsible for your child's emotional and economic support. Therefore, you will want to know as much as you can find out about how to handle this responsibility, so you can relax and enjoy it. You will want to do everything you can to discourage the view of mothers that says "you ought to be" this, or that, or the other thing, otherwise you aren't a good mother. A good mother can be any woman—whoever you are, whatever your situation. There is no one prescribed way for *everyone* to be a good mother.

TEENAGE MOTHERS

Whether *you* know anything about motherhood or not, whether *you* plan to have a baby or not, the fact is that a million teenagers will become pregnant this year. The number of single-parent families (99.4 percent are headed by women) is increasing faster than the statistics can be gathered and recorded. Many of these young mothers are high risks for abusing their children.

In many states the government won't pay for abortions even when our Supreme Court guarantees that right to all women. If you have a baby and have the money, often you can't find needed childcare for your young children. Many young mothers, who would like to, can't afford to stay home to care for their infants. These are scary situations for young mothers. Usually, we hear only the good things about motherhood, about how happy mothers are, how much they adore their children and how much others adore them too. About how *natural* it is to be a mother, she would be happy ever after.

But how about the practical side of the story? It doesn't sound so good to hear that mothers will have to be financially responsible for themselves and their babies. We aren't used to hearing of the father who leaves a young mother to fend for herself and her baby.

Until recently, not many young women did. But now, suddenly, many young women are responsible for their own young families *because* they are single. Often, even their parents won't help support them. When these young women are suddenly put in the position of supporting themselves *plus* their child or children, many are in shock that they can't get themselves together to do something constructive about it. Sometimes the shock and unbelievability of it all make them give up—give up to mental depression, suicide and child abuse.

Some young mothers are not left alone. They are married, but other problems can still take over. Following a husband wherever his career takes him, the realization after childbirth that they are responsible for their child for the next twenty years, accepting their mixed feelings about being a mother, finding ways to live a life as a mother, wife and employed woman; finding ways to make peace with their own mother and their husband's family—all these are things that can happen with motherhood that you don't hear much about before you get there. Usually, when people see the problems coming they can handle theirs better. This mother book will help you to see things coming.

When you see a variety of motherhood possibilities coming, you can better prepare *now,* in school, for your career. As soon as you accept the idea that motherhood is part of your career development—a place to learn transferable skills for later employment—then the years you are sharing with your babies are years that count as career-development time. Having a baby sooner than you had planned doesn't *have* to lead to unsolved problems. Working out decisions in your family, and noticing that family life changes as the baby changes and as you and your husband grow, will help you both cope with the specific problems of motherhood at a young age.

BE A MOTHER

You can learn to enjoy being a mother . . . no matter what. There just aren't any situations that can't be

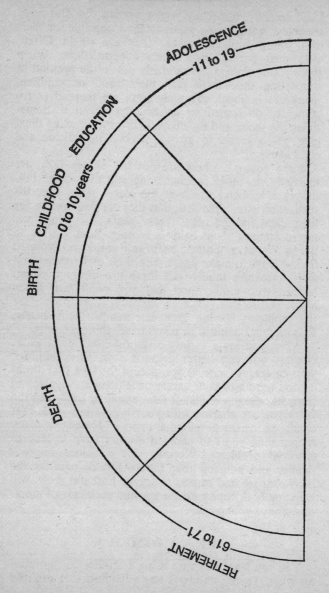

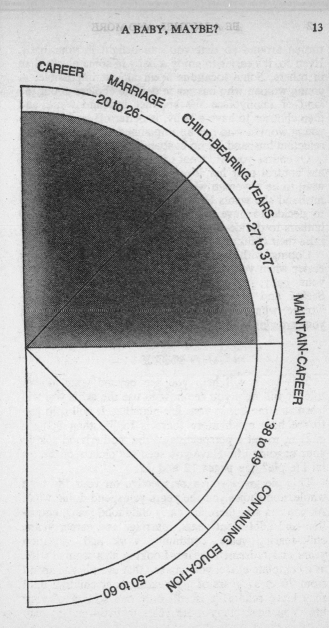

CAREER

MARRIAGE
20 to 26

CHILD-BEARING YEARS
27 to 37

MAINTAIN-CAREER

38 to 49

CONTINUING EDUCATION

50 to 60

turned around so that you can delight in your baby. Even so, it's easier to enjoy a baby in some places than in others. Some locations seem almost impossible. A young woman who has made definite choices about the kind of familyplace she and her husband want, and then chooses to have a baby, is better off by far than a young woman who has an unplanned pregnancy with a reluctant husband, or no husband at all in her life.

Of course you will want to be the young woman who has control over her life—who makes choices. You'll want to be a woman who bothers to decide the kind of husband she wants to build her life with, who bothers to decide to have sex that leads to pregnancy, who bothers to decide the kind of familyplace they want to raise their children in.

Coping with motherhood in a changing world is easier when you have some clues about taking care of your baby, emotionally, financially and physically. Seeing and accepting responsibilities in your familyplace, whatever that is like, helps you to grow with your growing child.

AND MORE . . .

This book will help you see beyond your mother role. It will help you see how to use the skills you will learn as a mother in your life-planning. It will help you to see how much more there is to life than being a mother, to get a perspective of the motherhood role in your ongoing life. Have you seen the picture of the total life pie? See pages 12 and 13.

This pie gives you a perspective on your life as a whole, and shows you the years you spend doing what. As you can see, there are early childhood years, education and adolescent years, marriage and career years, child-rearing years, continuing work and education years and retirement years. Looking at a woman's life as a complete circle, you can see that even if you spend from 20 to 37 years of age rearing your children until they leave school, it is still only one section of your life. You have many more years to live—and to plan for. Most young women, as you learned from the statistics of employed mothers, don't take 17 years off for childcare, so they have even more years to plan for outside their homes. In other words, even if your first goal is motherhood (and for many women it isn't) there is no way you can spend your whole life doing it.

To get a better idea about your total life, the things you have done—the experiences you enjoyed and those you didn't, fill in some of the specifics of your "pie of life." The words outside the circle are guidelines to help you fill in the details of your own pie, some of the things women experience as they build and plan their lives. Write in the things you expect to do and enjoy in your future years. Maybe the pie will help you see that, unlike what many young women are led to believe, motherhood is *not* an end in itself. Just like many of life's other experiences—high school, college, marriage, a job, a profession, motherhood leads to something else. But all of these things fit within an overall life, extending and overlapping each other. Thus your experiences build and blend, one into the other. As you develop skills through action and study, you can reflect on and reevaluate your growth, making changes in your life goals and activities as you go along. Wanting to be a mother, and being a good mother, should in no way take away from your need for decision-making about all the other roles and times in your life.

MAKING THE PIE

It's your pie. You can plan a recipe to mix your educational experiences with your work and play experiences (including motherhood). The whole pie is your career. As you develop skills in one area of your life you will want to see how they can be used in other parts of your life, transferring what you learn as you go along. Add the ingredients that you like, so that you can see how it looks and tastes and then make whatever changes you choose. You can't always change everything in the pie. For example, maybe you can't change the baby in your life, but you can change the time you spend with the baby, and you can design your life around the baby's growth from infant to toddler to school-age. You *can* plan now—to Be a Mother . . . and More.

TEENAGE SEXUALITY: RIGHTS AND RESPECT

"I finally told the admissions officer (sigh) . . . See, first of all I was suppose to start college late because I had mono, then I says I'd be kind of chicken to give him a medical report just on my mono—you know, I said I might just as well tell him. That I'm pregnant. And he had to read the note three times. To, you know, get it, 'cause it just really shocked him. It was a shock to everybody, you know? *She* was going to college.' I was the first in my family to ever even *want* to go to college.

"I never wanted children—and I still don't. It was just this thing, you know, it just happened. I want my career and I don't want anything to hold it back. When I was in high school schoolwork took all my time. I don't want to share my life with someone else. He didn't even turn me on! It never connected, I never thought of sex and pregnancy as the same thing."

—*Chris, a 7–months-pregnant teenager*

"A lot of my friends said that I was the last person in the world that they expected to get pregnant. I think it was because I have a career that I would like to be working on. Now I'm sitting around for nine months and it takes so long to pursue it because I am a musician and I want to be on the road. I sing. It was like—boy, how

dumb!—A lot of people would look at me and
say, "You're getting kind of fat for a singer, aren't
you?' And I'd say, 'That's not *fat*. I'm pregnant!'
It happened one of those times when we just
didn't bother to use anything. I thought, oh well,
it won't happen to me. There's no way *I* can get
pregnant—I'm too into my career."

—*Julie, a 9–months-pregnant teenager*

BOTHER TO DECIDE

If you are of child-bearing age and serious about
your life-planning, you have to admit that you are a
sexual being, regardless of what you do about it. You
have to *bother to decide* to have or not to have sex, to
use contraceptives, to abort or not if you get pregnant,
to give up your child for adoption or keep the baby.
You have to make these unique decisions about having
babies because you, and only you, actually carry and
have the baby. It's you who has to bother to decide
what you are going to do if you get pregnant.

ARE YOU A GAL WHO NEEDS
TO GET PREGNANT?*

1. Are you a gal who doesn't know the facts?
    a) I'm safe.
    b) I wasn't in love.
    c) I wasn't married.
    d) It was the first time.
    e) He pulled it out.
2. Are you a gal who wants to drop out from
    school?
    a) I don't like school.
    b) My boyfriend is working.
    c) I don't know what I want to be.
    d) School is boring.
    e) His place is more exciting than school.
    f) I can take care of myself.
3. Are you a gal who makes out in order to keep
    him?

*Adapted with permission from the author, Lise Brack-
ett (Toad Hollow Publishing).

a) Now he knows I love him.
b) Now he'll leave his wife.
c) He won't want to go with anyone else.
d) He said I'm the only one.
e) I won't get jealous because he is mine.
4. Are you a gal who is lonely?
a) I want a baby to love.
b) I want to be needed.
c) I'm too fat to be popular.
d) Nobody wants me.
e) I'm tired of putting out for nothing.
5. Are you a gal who wants to leave home?
a) My parents are too strict.
b) My parents don't care about me.
c) My parents don't trust me.
d) My parents don't like my friends.
e) I want my own place.
f) My brothers and sisters are driving me crazy!

If you are any one of these gals, you can be on the road to an early career in motherhood. It's easy for adults to give you advice. None of the statements under #1 are true. All of the situations will lead to pregnancy. Under #5 it's easier to leave home without a baby than with one. But most improtant is what you yourself *think* about these questions and attitudes. What do your friends think? Discuss the situations above with a friend or a group. Find out if you are a gal who *needs* to get pregnant.

YOU ARE A SEXUAL BEING

Parents and other adults often get so frightened at the thought of their children getting pregnant that they deny that they are sexual beings. From some parents' and teachers' attitudes about sexuality, it's often hard to realize that you are actually a sexual being from birth to death. You don't have to be sexually active to be a sexual being.

You are a sexual being before anyone asks you to share a sexual relationship. You are a sexual being whether you are asked or not. And you are the person who must deal with your sexuality, with intimate relationships, with contraceptives, with unwanted pregnancies, with abortions and with adoptions. It's one thing to know the biological facts about male and female differences, or likenesses, or enjoyment of sex, or needs and interests in sex but knowing those facts doesn't decide for you what you will actually do about sex.

Teenage sex is a problem for you because teenage pregnancy can be the consequence of this decision. It's a problem for you because you can keep your self-respect or lose it depending on the choices you decide to make. Your choices about sex are easier to make when you think of and consider other people in your life. Think about your boyfriend. Are you in a relationship with him, or is sex all you've got going? If you are in a relationship, what do the two of you want from each other besides sex? Would a relationship without sex work better for both of you right now? Simply knowing that you are a sexual being, and that no one can take your sexuality away from you regardless of how you express it, can be very helpful. You don't have to prove it, because *everybody* is a sexual being. You are also a being who needs self-respect. Most of us learn about and develop our self-respect through the people who are important to us. You can learn through your boyfriend. And your girlfriends. Through your parents and their friends, your teachers and other youth workers. Your cousins and aunts and uncles all contribute to your attitudes about yourself.

Many adults who are in professions that are supposed to be helping adolescent girls, have the misconception that today, because you have the pill, you have a new sexual freedom. New ways to prevent pregnancy do *not* give you sexual freedom! As long as you are doing sexually what the present sex image for women happens to be—whether that means being a virgin or being a sexual athlete—you don't have sexual freedom. Sexual freedom comes *only* when you decide for *yourself*—because *you* are a sexual being—what you are going to do. When *you* decide not to hop into bed with everyone who comes along and asks you, when *you* decide that you can initiate your own sexual relationships, when *you* decide never to have sex without protecting yourself from a possible pregnancy, when *you* decide to abstain altogether—*then* you have sexual freedom.

SEX EDUCATION AT HOME

Sexual freedom doesn't come from doing what other people want or value. Even though you may choose as others would, you still have to think through and live through the family and church and peer values that you have grown up with. Teens don't usually buy the values of their family completely, but they don't usually discount all of them either. High school and college years are times to explore your own feelings and ideas to make them fit into a value system of your own. Sexual freedom, like intellectual freedom, means working things out that are right for you.

Many parents are notorious for completely ignoring your sexuality, as if it could be separated out of your life from your educational and career planning and decision-making. You sometimes hear that parents are against sex education and teaching you about birth control because they think if you teach a kid the truth about sex, she'll go out and do it. One junior in high school disagrees: "The less you're aware of sex, the more exciting it becomes and then you have to learn it all on your own." A lot of high school students say they wish they could talk about sex with their parents. It isn't just a matter of talking about anatomy and the biological reproductive system and birth control, they say. It's attitudes about sex, and myths about sex, and the sexual behavior of young women and men that many teens would like to know more about. Every generation of young people has found it hard to talk about their sex feelings with their parents.

Maria, a 9-months-pregnant teenager says:

> "Well, my mother and I talked but, you know, she never told me about the birds and the bees . . . and things like that. I actually told my older sisters about it. You know my mother, she

was kind of self-conscious about talking about things like that. Adults should pound it into our heads that we have to use contraceptives. Well, I had heard that but they didn't really say you have to use them *all* the time. It's one of those things that aren't talked about. Like I heard about it in general but I never really associated getting pregnant with sex. I saw them as two totally different things, you know? One didn't have anything to do with the other. So I just never bothered with it, you know, but it should be taught. It should be taught that pregnancy does go along with sex if there is no contraceptive used. My mother never . . . she didn't like the pill, she hates the pill, and she always said to me, you know, if you ever have to use birth control, don't take the pill. And like, what else is there?"

One way for you to take the initiative and try to start a conversation with your parents about sex is by asking questions. Such as: Did you nurse me when I was first born? Did you enjoy it? Did I enjoy getting hugged? Did I ask for backrubs? Did you used to be like me? Did you go steady in junior high school? How did you feel about sex when you were in high school? In college?

Another way to get a conversation going is to give one or both of your parents something to read that *you've* read about teenagers and sexuality. One book to start with is this one! Two others books are listed at the end of this section on page 25. Look at these books for opinions, questions and discussions about some of the doubts and fears about sexuality that hit every young person growing up.

One reason it's so important for you to talk about sex to your parents or other trusted adults is because adults often assume you know a lot more about sex and sexuality and contraception than you actually may know.

Some of you, of course, will *not* find your parents or other adults at all willing to talk about sex. It's harder for you in that case, but you still owe it to yourself to learn all you can about sex. Others of you will try to cover up your lack of sex information in order to appear more grown-up. Don't get into the "I know the facts *at my age*" attitude, like Marcia below, and miss out on asking questions and discussing the things you *really* need to know.

Marcia is a college drop-out who went off the pill before she found out how people get pregnant. Here's what she said:

> "I was kind of in a situation where, well, I was on the pill, but I wasn't exactly sure what for. OK, I knew it was so I wouldn't get pregnant, so I wouldn't have a baby, but how was *I* going to have a baby??? You know, I'm serious, that shows you how naive I was, and I was eighteen! I was informed. I was going to Planned Parenthood, and they said, 'Here, take these pills so you don't get pregnant.' But *how* was I going to get pregnant . . ." My aunt said, 'Hey look, you're going to college. Get on the pill so you won't get pregnant . . .'
>
> "And I didn't want to ask because they weren't telling me anything except I had to take the pill so I wouldn't get pregnant. I was on the pill about a year before I had sex. I went to college and listened to the other kids. I didn't ask about it; there was nothing to ask. I didn't know what was going on. I was at a stage where nothing surprised me . . . It was a whole new different thing; I was just taking all of this in. My older sister told me I was a fool, you know, if I went to college without going on the pill. That's what puzzled me. My sister said, 'Don't think you are going to college and those boys are going to keep their hands off you. You are going to get tangled up with somebody.'"

SEX EDUCATION AT SCHOOL

Maybe you had a sex-education unit in school way back when, and the information they gave you didn't really sink in. Maybe you're like the 9th-grader from an exclusive private day-school in New York City who responded to "have you had sex education in school?" with "Oh yes, we had it in the fifth grade." "Did they talk about contraceptives in the fifth grade? "I don't remember."

Or maybe you're like Nina, a 4-months-pregnant 9th grader who had a sex-education unit in a health class:

> "I took sex-ed in health class. I was the only girl in a room full of boys, and it's kind of hard to concentrate on contraceptives and stuff when you're sitting in a room full of boys. (Laughs.) A couple of other girls started in the class but they dropped out; they couldn't handle it with all the boys in there. They went through all the contraceptives but all that information wasn't doing anything. It was just sitting up there. (Points to head, laughs.) It never really penetrated my brain. It was impersonal because I was a sophomore and, you know, I wasn't having sex then. And so I just, I never needed it. It didn't store it in my memory. It just didn't register . . . Nothing about that class registered when I needed it."

Nina was asked, "If you had a thirteen-year-old sister, and she was going steady but you knew she didn't have any sexual life with her boyfriend yet, what would you tell her about contraceptives?"

Nina replied, "I'd slap her and tell her that's an awful dumb thing to do!"

"And if you were the younger, thirteen-year-old sister and your older sister slapped you and said that to you, what would you say?"

"I'd tell her to mind her own business!"

Deciding to have sex *is* your own business—it's a private decision. But getting pregnant becomes other people's business—it's a public issue. That's why schools and churches and other adult groups are interested in your sex education. Because it affects us all. Bringing a new baby into the world and creating a new family has an impact on a lot of your relatives and the father's relatives. Once the baby is born it becomes the responsibility of the childcare center, the government, the school system and the church, anywhere and everywhere you take it.

Learning the facts you need to know about sex, and letting the information sink in so that it's a part of you when you need it most—which is at the time of deciding what to do about *having* sex, is what you need to do now.

MORE TO READ ABOUT SEX

Love and Sex in Plain Language by Eric W. Johnson, revised 1979, Bantam. A traditional view of complete sex information for teens.

Sex, With Love by Eleanor Hamilton, 1979, Beacon Press. A liberal view of sex for sophisticated teens.

SEXUAL MYTHS

Talking about the myths of sex can be a good way to discuss sex at home with your parents or with other interested adults. Myths are important to discuss because they often support the barriers that keep you from accepting your sexuality.

Anything that's kept as secret as sex has to have myths surrounding it. And the sooner you can separate fact from myth, the sooner you can get rid of your false fears about sex and be aware of the real sexual problems for teenagers. One danger from myths is that they give you false information. Another danger is that myths often make you feel as if what you are thinking and doing is wrong. Sometimes they may even make you feel as though something's the matter with you. The goal in learning more about sexuality is to learn to accept your sexual feelings, no matter what they are. Accepting your sexual feelings has nothing to do with what you'll actually decide to *do* with your feelings. But learning about myths means you have a place to start when you know how *you* feel, rather than how your family, or teachers or friends feel. A good place to begin to talk about sexual myths is with:

THE MASTURBATION MYTHS

Because parents have often acted as though you aren't supposed to have sexual feelings until marriage, and because sexual feelings start at a very young age, the masturbation myths outnumber most of the others. Masturbation scares parents and teachers because it proves that you are indeed a sexual being—even years before marriage. The following statements based on myths are familiar scare tactics to force children to stop masturbating: "You'll go blind." "You'll go crazy." "You won't enjoy sex in marriage." "You'll get pimples if do." "You'll weaken your brain and your college board scores will go down." "People can tell by looking in your eyes if you do." "God will punish you."

With this list of myths it's a wonder that anyone does it. You often hear, however, that masturbation is a good way to learn about your sexual responses and often leads to good preparation for sex with a partner.

THE FANTASY MYTHS

"Only men have sexual fantasies." "You never need to fantasize if you are with a real person, or with the one you love." "Fantasy means that's what you really want to do." "Fantasies are abnormal." "They are disloyal to the people you love."

Nonsense! Fantasies are a rich, pleasurable and healthy part of sexuality. Some fantasies are fun and some are frightening. They do not represent at all what a person would actually do, or even wants to do. They are purely in your head, not something that should worry you. Anybody who fantasizes about anything, fantasizes about sex. Unlike actions, any fantasy is OK.

THE LESBIAN MYTHS

"If you love another woman, you will never be able to love a man." "Lesbians are afraid of men." "Lesbians wish they were men." "Lesbians are sick." "Lesbians will outgrow this phase of sexual development."

The scare tactics in this case have to do with your not being "right" if you can live without a man. Because of the cultural pressures to conform to the role of a married person with children, many women and men don't have a clue whether they are asexual, bisexual, homosexual or whatever-sexual. The crucial task for you is to notice what and who turns you on (even though it isn't accepted or valued by others), and to learn to accept and trust whatever you learn about your sexuality. As you learn to be conscious of your sexual feelings, it's very important for you to know also that you can choose *not* to act on them. Because another young woman turns you on, you don't have to choose to make love with her, just as you don't go to bed with every guy who turns you on, or with the people about whom you fantasize. Learning about your feelings is not the same as deciding what you choose to do about your feelings.

Your closest friends are probably your female friends. Being close to your friends doesn't mean you are a lesbian. Be as open as you can in all of your relationships and try to live by your experiences—not the myths.

THE VIRGINITY MYTHS

"No man wants secondhand goods." "If you sleep with a man he'll never marry you." "A bride's virginity is her most precious treasure." "A man should have experiences, a woman should have innocence." "If you don't have a hymen, you're not a virgin." "If you don't bleed on your first intercourse, you don't have a hymen." "First intercourse is painful." "First intercourse is heavenly and something you can only have once, so save it for your future husband."

The whole mythical concept of virginity is a good example of how women have traditionally thought of themselves as belonging to men, letting sex just happen to them rather than having it be something that is in their own interest. The virginity myths are a powerful force that have been constructed and shaped by others—parents, men, the church, and the offshooting values of our culture—not by women themselves. Now that it is fashionable for men to want experienced women, sex is viewed as a move from childhood to adulthood, a definite breaking away from parents and toward independence. Independence is a good thing, but sex before you are ready for it is a high price to pay.

The present-day idea of who should be a virgin should not be taken as seriously as your understanding of where you are and what you want. What you decide to do about sex this year may change next year. Deciding not to have sex right now doesn't mean you are frigid, or that no one can turn you on. It just means that, turned on or not, you have your reasons not to have sex at this particular time.

THE CONTRACEPTIVE MYTHS

"Saran-wrap prevents pregnancy." "You don't get pregnant when you are menstruating." "Withdrawal (of the penis just before orgasm) prevents pregnancy." "The best contraceptive is denial, withdrawal and hope." "You have to do it more than once to get pregnant." "Only French kissing gets you pregnant." "You won't get pregnant if you don't come to orgasm." "If your hymen is intact, you can't get pregnant." "You won't get pregnant if you are not in love."

None of these myths are true. Women get pregnant regardless of all of the above myths. There are all kinds of books about contraception and birth control. The two books mentioned earlier on page 25 are good examples. Look in the library card catalogue under "birth control" for others. Look in your telephone book under "Planned Parenthood" for an agency that provides information on birth control to young women. You don't need your parents' permission to use these aids, you don't need to be married and you don't need to see a doctor first. They help teens and single women with questions that are hard to ask and discussions that are hard to get started. It's easy to get the facts about birth control. It's not so easy to figure out why some young women use birth control and others don't. There are a lot of outdated attitudes and values that keep you from protecting yourself from an unwanted pregnancy.

"I DON'T USE THEM."

"I wasn't using anything—and he wasn't either. Oh God—yes, I feel very lucky not to have gotten pregnant. I just learned about all that stuff and I'm going on the pill as soon as I can. I've got this younger friend who is thirteen and she doesn't use any birth control either—because she knows I don't. Before I knew about it, I told her *none* of us can get pregnant—like it isn't goin' to happen to us! Well, my cousin was in our group too and she kept saying, 'I won't get pregnant, I won't get pregnant,' and, a little later, 'Cynthia, I'm pregnant!' (Groans.)"

This was the experience of Cynthia, a sexually active 15-year-old.

Probably the most common reason why a young woman doesn't use contraceptives is because she really doesn't believe that she will get pregnant. Or perhaps she just isn't thinking about pregnancy, she is thinking about sex. Or maybe thinking about her boyfriend and how she's getting along with him. Another big reason on the top of the list of reasons why teenage girls don't use birth control is because sex isn't planned ahead. Sex doesn't always happen with a steady boyfriend, but might just happen with someone you haven't talked with that much. You are at a party, say, or on a date and you just want to see how it goes. There is no concern about unprotected sex because your thoughts are on the excitement of what is going on with that guy—right then.

Here are more reasons sexually active teens have given for not using contraceptives:

"To buy contraceptives is to admit that I am going to have sexual relations. If I'm not sure it's right I just let sex happen, passion takes over and planning ahead of time is the last thing on my mind."

"Talking about birth control and planning with my boyfriend takes the romance out of sex. Sex is beautiful, spontaneous, uncontrollable and spiritual."

"My boyfriend doesn't like birth control. If I am just starting to make love, I'd never say, 'Let's wait until we have birth control,' because he might decide not to make love with me at all. He would tell the other guys what a jerk I am."

"I know more about contraceptives than my boyfriend but we don't discuss it because it makes him feel not as smart as I am about sex."

"Sometimes I do it to see what will happen. I wonder how many times I can have sex before I get pregnant. I wonder if I *can* get pregnant."

"I'm not supposed to be having sex. My mother would kill me if she thought I was using birth control."

"I don't take birth control because it's not safe. It's safer to be pregnant than to take birth control."

"I USE THEM."

Here are some very good reasons given by teens for using contraceptives:

"I want to try sex because I have sexual feelings and a steady boyfriend. I feel that I have as much right to sex as my boyfriend does."

"I respect the guy I am having sex with. I don't want to trap him into the complexities of fatherhood before he is ready."

"I respect new human beings and I will wait to bring a new one into the world until I am ready to be responsible for it."

"I respect my parents' efforts to give me a good beginning in life. I don't want to disappoint them with a pregnancy."

"I have plans for my life and those plans include a sexually active life, but my plans do not include an unplanned pregnancy."

Sexually active teens must have protected sex. A sexually active teenager has to protect herself *always* because she does *not* want to hurt herself, her family or her boyfriend with an unplanned baby. Birth control is a matter of the rights and respect you have for yourself, the respect you have for the unborn, the respect you have for others in your life, and the respect you expect from others.

TEENAGE SEX LIFE

A lot of adults think that today's young women have much less fear of pregnancy, and much more fun with sex, since the pill and the easier access to abortion. What they don't realize is that a lot of young women who are into a sexual life aren't happily into sex. "I said I did it, I didn't say I enjoyed it," was the comment given by one sexually active 15-year-old in an interview.

Recent research on teenage sexuality by the International Woman's Year Committee shows that young women who start a sexual life early, do not continue happily ever after. They start and stop. Many do it once to say they did it. They want to find out what it's all about and be able to tell their friends about it, and then they stop for a couple of years.

Here are some comments of Barby, a 15-year-old single mother of a 4-day-old baby:

"I thought sex was a real hassle, but it was the normal thing to do—so I did it. Now I don't care what society thinks. If I don't want to go out for sex, then I won't. It's nobody's business. Everybody kept saying, 'Oh, you are going to like it, you are going to like it.' Friends, parents, social workers, doctors, were all encouraging me to be 'normal.' Now I'd just as soon be a little less normal."

Like other "adult only" activities and behavior, sex is something that everyone wants to try. But unlike other adult activities, sex can have consequences for someone else—the unborn. Many of you have access to contraceptives and know more about them than your parents do. Yet even young women who know about contraceptives are getting pregnant in rapid numbers—more than one million a year, leading to some 350,000 abortions and many more unwanted babies. It often seems that there is a race going on—a race to see who is going to have sex first.

When asked why they tried sex so early, many young women replied, "Because it's so easy." Their parents are both away perhaps, and no one is home. Often the parents are divorced and sometimes even more preoccupied with sex than their children are. Boyfriends and girlfriends are left alone in the house together and sex is something new and easy to try in a home where no supervision exists. This kind of situation often creates a snowball effect. Young teens get married and divorced even sooner than their parents did, and then their children start all over again with even earlier sex, earlier marriage—and earlier divorces.

TEENAGE PREGNANCY

Who gets pregnant?

You have probably read in your local newspapers, the weekly news magazines and your own teen magazines that there are one million teenage pregnancies a year. The International Women's Year Committee recently gathered facts on teenage pregnancies and here they are. About a quarter of these pregnancies (27 percent) are terminated by abortion. But in addition, 125,000 teenagers who wanted abortions were not able to get them. Of the over half a million who had their babies (600,000 15-to-19-year-olds; 30,000 12-to-15-year-olds; and 13,000 under-12-year-olds, almost all (9 out of 10) kept their babies.

These pregnancies happen to teenagers because 11 million 15-to-19-year-olds are sexually active, another million 13-to 14-year-olds are sexually active, and most of them do not use contraceptives. Most were told about birth control by their parents. Of all the sexually active young women one-fourth of them didn't know it was possible to get pregnant during a single act of intercourse (any time in your menstrual cycle), and almost one-third (30 percent) didn't know where to get contraceptives.

What do all of these facts about teenage sex and pregnancy mean to you? Sex is a problem! And it's a problem because of the constant conflict between discovering something new, something fun, something great (even though sometimes frustrating), and the tragic consequences sex can bring to young women—an unplanned pregnancy. The taboo parents and adults put on teenage sexuality, on your emotions, or sexual urges, and on your struggles with intimate relationships, and plus the pressures from young men to have sex in order to prove their masculinity, are all part of the conflict.

Many adults either ignore the sexuality of their children, hoping it will go away, or they insist that sex is only for married couples with meaningful relationships. The difficulty for teenagers is that pregnancy can and does occur whether you have meaningful sex relationships or not! Pregnancy can easily happen the first time—and often does. Often the first sex experience occurs as a result of curiosity, or persuasion, or trying to get back at your parents, or maybe just runaway emotions of the moment. Starting a baby may be the last thing on your mind—at that time.

WILL YOU BOTHER TO DECIDE ABOUT HAVING SEX?

Most teenage pregnancies occur because the women did not bother to decide. You cannot decide your sexual behavior by the standards of what society says a young woman should or should not do. Sexual decisions cannot be separated out and decided on as if they stand alone. One way to think about sex decisions is to think about the kinds of friendships you want right now, and how these friendships support you or don't support you, encourage you or discourage you.

It's not easy at any age to build friendships that involve sex. But it seems to be even harder for teenagers. Young women are systematically taught that what men say has more authority—that men know more than women, that they need and like sex more than women, and that if you really love your boyfriend, you will express that love through sex. It never occurs to many of you to say if they really love *you,* they wouldn't push it if you weren't ready! Or you may try to get your boyfriend interested in you sexually just to see if you're attractive—and then not know how to get out of the situation when you succeed. Our culture has set things up so that it's a contest and game for a young man to score, to see how many women he can make out with, and for young women to see how many young men they can attract. Often, even though it isn't fair, the burden is on the young women to decide, because the guy has *already* decided he is pushing for a sexual relationship. Most often it's you who has to decide about contraceptives, and to take the consequences if it results in a pregnancy.

EQUAL PARTNERS

One way out of this problem—if you are going to be sexually active—is to try to be an equal partner. Get your boyfriend into some of the problems. Discuss and talk about them. Expect him to be interested enough in your relationship to plan ahead for sex (always using contraceptives)—if you are into sex.

If you see yourself as an equal partner in your friendship—then you will feel that you have the right, and enough respect from him, to say, "No—not unless we're protected from pregnancy *every time.*" If you are sure of your right to say so, if you respect yourself and your boyfriend, if you are sure of what you want to do sexually, you will *always* abstain from sex—or use contraceptives. But like many adult women, you may often treat your body as if it belonged more to your boyfriend, to his wants and needs and curiosity, then to yourself.

How then can you decide? The best sex has to do with relationship. Talk it over with him. Spend some time and thought on what you want from your boyfriend right now, and how that will fit in with the rest of your life. Your school and home life. Your sports. Your girlfriends, and the other guys as well. Keep in mind, too, that you will decide one thing now, and then perhaps decide something different as the situation changes. As your boyfriend changes, as you change boyfriends, as you yourself change and grow, as your needs become different, as you understand where you are going, as you make other commitments. You can change your mind at any time. As long as you respect yourself enough to protect yourself, you can keep your choices and options always open. You can try new things or decide not to and focus instead on something else. It's your body. It's your life. *You* can bother to decide what's most important to you as you plan it.

~~§ • ?~~

CHILDFREE OR CHILDCARE

CHILDFREE

Some of you reading this book will choose *not* to be mothers. It may sometimes be hard to believe, with all the media pressure about what a happy family is like, and what you should do—and buy—to be part of such a family, but it *is* possible to be a grownup, happy and successful woman without being a mother!

You may have already noticed some of the obvious pressures to have a baby that young women and girls are subject to as they grow up:

To have something of your own.

To have a love object.

To have someone who you think will always love you.

To give a grandchild to your parents.

To be needed.

To have something worthwhile to do.

To help a bad marriage.

To give direction to your life.

To give your child things you never had.

To carry on your life after you've gone.

To prove your husband is a real man.

To prove you are a real woman.

The fact is, for the first time in history, there are a great many women who feel strongly that motherhood is not the only purpose in life for a woman. These women, who have decided not to have a child, have

36

been able to pull it off because of improved contraceptives and an understanding partner. Diane and David are one couple who decided to have a childfree family.

David, 27, and Diane, 26, have been students together, workers together, and they have worked to support each other. Neither has strong career goals, neither wants a baby, at least not now; neither is worried.

Married almost five years, they are concerned now with staying together, living in California and having a good time. There are no immediate plans for children. Diane, who graduated from college in 1977 and works as a waitress, said she hopes eventually to work "for enjoyment and satisfaction." She is in no hurry. David, who plays guitar with bands when he has the chance, said he is waiting for the right career opportunity to come along.

"I don't have any driving ambitions now. If I didn't need money to stay alive, I'd have one grand ol' time. It's just too hard today for two people to make it unless both of them work," said David, who enjoys his job as a maintenance man in an apartment building.

The problem with holding down two jobs is time, they said. Diane works nights and weekends; David works days and during the week. They like to go sailing and fly-fishing. Lately, each has done it alone. Sometimes they are able to rearrange schedules to be together. Since their present situations may change, the couple is not worried about long-term separations.

When they were first married, they took turns working. Diane said that the person who worked envied the one who didn't, even though the one at home did most of the domestic chores. "I'd get laid off from construction jobs and take a vacation," David said. "I guess it bothered me some when she was working to support me. I always expected my wife would work, but not forever and not because she needed to."

"Since the age of ten I knew I would go to college and be an art teacher. Now my peers and parents are pressuring me to get a job in the field I was trained for, or to have a baby," said Diane. "But once I start, I'll be doing that forever."

If David and Diane are having problems combining marriage and jobs, they do not talk about it. They do talk about shared priorities: living in California; having time to spend with each other, close friends and hobbies, such as music and sailing. Having children or challenging careers is not on their priority list. Work means money. Two workers means twice as much money to spend on good times.

In a world which thinks that having babies is best for all families, you don't need to search for reasons to have one. But if you decide *not* to have a baby, everyone will want to know why. Childfree families offer some of these reasons: over-population; a good career beginning; a lack of fondness for children and the wish not to spend time with them; a good relationship with a spouse and a life they don't want to change in any way (such as David and Diane). Others say the world is changing too fast and a lousy place for children anyway, what with the radiation and nuclear-bomb scares. Still others feel that they don't want to bring a child into the world and put it into some church basement for childcare all day. It takes a brave woman and a support group which can include a husband or friend or family to go against society's idea of what a young woman should be or do. If you are one of the young women who have decided not to be a mother, or who are at least asking the question, "Shall I have a baby?" there are pre-parenthood counseling services you can visit to help you. An excellent one in New York City is called a Baby? . . . Maybe. And the National Organization for Non-Parents (NON) is a support group for couples who choose not to have a baby.

DECIDING—NOW OR LATER

"Do I want to have a baby?" is the first question. *"If I have a baby, when will I have it?"* comes next. There is no reason to think that a baby has to follow within a year after marriage. If you have a "working things out" relationship with your husband, if you understand that family planning means more than a contraceptive system, then you can make a definite decision about when a baby would best fit into your life. "Family planning" means how does a baby fit into your marriage and career plans. When would a baby be a physical, emotional and financial drain that takes away from the joys and rewards of being a wife? When could you give most to a baby?

As your career and your love for your husband grow, you may change your mind and reevaluate. Many years may go by before you actually do decide that the best time has come for you and your husband to have a baby. Meg and Jay wanted to get a good start in their careers before they began their family:

Their kitchen floor is never very clean. There is not much time to relax in the evening and they often forfeit Saturday afternoons to do grocery shopping.

Otherwise, Meg and Jay have managed marriage and two fulltime careers with ease. After December, they expect to be managing marriage, jobs and a baby.

"We'd like to have more time, especially with the baby," said Jay, 30, an assistant attorney general and chief of the state's antitrust division. "The ideal situation would be two permanent parttime positions, each with 30 hours a week. I can't imagine either of us staying home all day, all year."

Meg, 27, is an assistant editor for publications at a university extension service and experiment station. The university, she said, has allowed her up to a year's maternity leave and guaranteed that she will be reinstated in the same position. She hopes to take a three-month leave when the baby is born, then go back to work on a parttime basis, and within the year, to return fulltime.

A close friend, whose baby will be born one month earlier, will care for their baby during the day.

Neither doubted that Meg would work and keep working. She has worked steadily since college, finds her career "Challenging, fulfilling . . . and just as important as Jay's." Jay is not yet ready for a paternity leave, however. He said it is not feasible for him now. "Society is just about ready for the working mother. Talk about paternity leaves and you get incredible stares."

Meg and Jay come from families which encouraged achievement. They both graduated from competitive, prestigious colleges where men and women students were expected to excel, get into good graduate schools and get good jobs. The women's liberation movement, Meg said, tended to reinforce the beliefs she already held.

"My own father never lifted a dish," she said. "When we were first married, I felt very strongly about avoiding traditional housewife roles. If I cooked Monday night, he had to do the dishes."

"We traded and bargained so much it began to get ridiculous," said Jay, whose mother, a school secretary, loves her job and worked fulltime while she reared her children.

After four years of marriage, Meg said she no longer feels she has to prove anything. Now they share responsibilities. If she drives by the cleaners, she picks up the clothes. If there is a meat special in town, he does the shopping.

In a few years, Meg plans to go to graduate school. Although Jay is not ready to become a house-husband, he is willing to relocate for Meg's job or education—provided there are opportunities there for him.

Meg and Jay said their marriage and mutual happiness always take precedence over their careers. Like the others, too, they said two jobs have helped financially.

"We can enjoy our life more and afford to do the extra things," said Jay, "like going out and taking vacations. We don't have to scrimp and save."

"We're fortunate," Meg said. "We're not doing this (work) because we have to. We have the careers that we want."

Just as Meg and Jay looked at their career development—where they were in their school or job, what they wanted to have achieved when Meg got pregnant, where they wanted to live, what kind of financial situation they wanted to be in—you too can consider and plan for all the things that will help make it possible to enjoy your baby if and when you finally have one. That's called family planning.

It used to be that first-time mothers over 30 were considered oddities. But those days have vanished. With more women marrying later, working longer and delaying childbirth until the mid- or late thirties, the rate of first births for women 30 to 34 has risen to 8.9 per 1,000, according to the National Center for Health Statistics. And even more important, it's a trend that is growing.

Women who have their first baby in their thirties say they are much more sure of themselves. Their attitude is well illustrated by one mother who had her first baby at 38 and who said, "Mothers in their twenties are competing in the park as to how old their children were when they were toilet trained and when they walked. But at my age you don't give a damn. Everyone walks or talks eventually. No one goes to college still tugging on a bottle."

There will always be many more mothers who have their babies when they are young. Some of you will have your family while you are in your late teens and early twenties, and your children will have grown up and gone by the time you are 37. Thirty-seven may seem a long way off to you right now, but take a look around you at women you know who are 37 and you'll notice that they've got a lot of years left to plan for. If you think about the life pie, you will see that at 37 you will have 28 years before retirement, before you're 65. Twenty-eight years is time worth planning for.

Marjorie is a good example of a woman who is very excited about her career plans at 37. Her second and last child left home this year. She has had her family, cared for them, seen them safely on their way to their own lives. She says, "I wouldn't have it any other way. I like the feeling of finishing one career before starting another one, rather than trying to integrate making money with raising children and being with them. With the children gone, I feel utterly free to give full attention to my money-making career."

As more women are choosing to have children later in life, more are deciding to have only one child (61 percent of first-time mothers over 30 plan to have only one). About the myth that it's hard on a child to be raised alone, Dr. Lee Salk, author of child-development books, writes, "For every single child I've seen who wanted a brother or sister, I know ten others who had them and wished they didn't." Single children often get more parental attention and a more realistic, more mature love. As adults they have a greater tendency to achieve, to earn more and to hold more prestigious jobs.

You have a lot of options for deciding when to have a baby. Getting married does not have to mean getting pregnant. Planning to have a baby any time between the ages of 20 and 40 gives you the control you need for planning your life. Looking at motherhood as *part* of your life rather than as the single reason for your life, just as your boyfriends and brothers look at fatherhood as only a part of their lives, may help you to see the need for career and family planning.

DECISIONS CHANGE

You may join the childfree group of families for a few years and then decide to have children later. You may have very good reasons not to have children, and those reasons may change, or your values and your priorities may change. All of these things influence your decision about whether to have children—and when.

Get your own reasons together about whether and when children would be best in your life. Changing your mind is a part of this process too. Changing your decision because you and your husband change is a healthy part of growing and decision-making.

CHILDBIRTH

Just as you can choose whether or not to have a baby, you can choose, also, the kind of childbirth that will be best for you and your husband. Being aware of the childbirth choices is the first step in making childbearing a good experience for you.

"IF I HAVE A BABY, WHO WILL CARE FOR IT?"

The simple answer that "mother" will care for the baby doesn't seem as simple as it used to. When we know that 41 percent of all mothers with children under six, and that 58 percent of all mothers with school-age children are working out of their homes on a fulltime basis, then we know also that a lot of women are asking the question, "Who will care for my baby?" We know also that women work because, just like men, they need the money. Chances are that you, too, may be looking for someone to care for your baby, because like other women, you will need to work.

A CHILD'S NEEDS

What do you know about children and their care in order to decide who will provide for them? Let's start with the child's needs. There are some things we do know about every baby's needs.

First of all, we know that babies need care 24 hours a day. Once you have a baby, there's no relief from that responsibility of caring for and supervising the baby *at all times*. If you aren't there to do it, you will have to find someone who will be there. You can't go to a movie, or run to the store, and leave an infant or toddler alone. Why? Simply because the dangers from fire, or strangers, or choking, or other sudden emergencies are present all the time. It is fulfilling this responsibility to provide constant care for a dependent that feels so good to many others—the feeling of being needed.

Second, all babies need a loving, trustworthy relationship with a primary caregiver. That doesn't have to be just one person, but it does mean that while the baby is under three, the fewer the better. It's easier for the baby to become attached to a few people than a whole group of caregivers. It isn't necessary to have the same person care for the baby all the time, but it is important that the caregivers are small enough in number for the baby to enjoy.

Betty, a school counselor, is very happy about the caregiver for her baby. She tells us: "Even though Jennie had Mike eight hours a day, my husband I were the primary caregivers of our baby. My feeling was that Mike had a third parent in Jennie, and she was a person that he did learn to trust and feel close to, just as he did with his father and me. Obviously he preferred to be with my husband and me."

And another professional mother, Annette, has this to say about her 2-year-old's caregiver: "Mary Jane is a very important person in his life. She has been Teddy's prime caregiver at the center since he was two months old until he was sixteen months old. And now he is in with another caregiver and he has adjusted beautifully. I thought, gee, he is going to miss Mary Jane since he's been with her five days a week, and I thought the transition is really going to be hard on him. But he was ready for it. He was ready for the new activities of the two-year-old and he enjoys them."

Annette continued: "I feel very good about the relationship I've got with Teddy at this point. I think it was the time that I spent with him. If I was always with him but didn't have time for his needs, and I was always doing something else, versus the time I have with him as it is, thinking this is *his* time, nothing else can go to this time. We didn't get dinner because that was his time so we made dinner later. I think that in only a few months he identified who I was after spending a full day with Mary Jane. I felt very good when we went into the daycare center and I said, "Teddy, there's Mary Jane!" And he really was excited about being with her. If you go with what some people say about it, you'd think that the kids wouldn't want to be with the caregivers if they were happy at home. I just haven't found this true."

Many employed parents feel that the other adult in their children's lives enriches their lives and their children's, and in no way takes away from the joys of being a parent.

Babies need the feeling of safety and security in their daily lives that comes from a routine, from a predictable schedule of activities and relationships. Babies need stimulating surroundings that reward them with good feelings and make them feel free to explore. They need love that they can draw on when they are in stress during difficult times. Fewer caregivers make it easier for the baby to establish her roots in her family, to draw on the family's strengths expressed in caring for the baby. A small group gives the baby time to feel a part of a family group before going out into larger groups.

Many mothers know what's best for their baby, but they just can't work it out that way. Theresa knew it was important for her baby to be with someone good but she just couldn't pull it off. When she returned to her cashier's job after her baby was born, she first tried leaving the baby with her cousin. But that arrangement didn't work out and within two months she had to leave the baby with the woman across the street. Very soon the woman decided to go out to work herself and the third arrangement within three months was for a woman to come in and care for the baby. Theresa soon found she couldn't really afford the woman coming to her home, plus the baby was upset and irritable a lot of the time and was developing a sleeping problem. So Theresa finally just gave up and decided to go on welfare until her baby was old enough for school. She hated to go on welfare, but she valued even more giving her baby a good start in life with one adult—herself.

One mother who is also a nurse tells what the daily routine is like for Sue, her 2-year-old: "I have her an hour in the morning before we leave the house. We usually arrive at the center at seven-thirty or seven-forty and I spend the time I need to before I leave. Sue has no problem with separation. She expects me to leave. When she was seven or eight months old to about a year and a half, I had to spend more on activities with her before I left. I would play with her, getting her involved with something or with one of the caregivers, and then I could just fade out of the scene. Now, at twenty-three months, I just drop Sue off and she doesn't seem to need the extra time. I pick her up between four-thirty and five, we get home about five and she goes to bed at eight. Her father often gives Sue a bath at night and rocks her at rocking time. The time with her in the evening seems quite precious to us, but when eight o'clock comes I'm really ready to put her into bed!"

THE PARENTS' NEEDS

It's not always possible to be at home with your baby. Marie is an employed mother and she expresses her feelings about her needs like this: "I can see from the time I had with Laurie that I personally would not be able to be at home all the time. I wouldn't like it. I love children and I love my work, but I can see that I wouldn't be a very happy person if I had to choose between them. I think that I have a lot to offer my profession, and that's where I want to be. I mean, I haven't even finished paying my school debt, and I would feel horrible if I were home knowing that I wanted to be working in my profession. And if I were still paying for my education and didn't have the opportunity, I would be a very unhappy person. And I don't think the time I'd give to my chidren would be as high in quality as it is now."

For some mothers, it *is* possible to be at home caring for the baby, and that's exactly where they want to be. Gail has a baby and a 4-year-old and she finds that the time she puts in with her children makes her feel better than time spent anywhere else. Gail says, "I used to work, but it just didn't have the meaning that being with my children has. I was an accountant, I enjoyed my work, I liked being out with other people, but something was missing. I knew that a hundred others could handle my accountant's work and I didn't feel special. At home with my two children makes me really feel needed. I love the time with them. I like their constant questions, I like thinking of things for them to do, I love teaching them about what's going on in the world. Childcare in *my* family means me!"

Even if you are employed fulltime, keeping in mind that the fewer primary caretakers the better, try to arrange your work or school and parenting life so that you can be with your infant as much as possible until he is 3.

Diane is a good example of a mother who arranged to be with her baby at crucial times. She had her son in the infant-care center where she was employed, and this is how it worked out: "I have always considered myself the primary caregiver for Shawn. Up until he was six months old, he would be breast-fed at noon, and I'd go and get him and take him for my whole lunch hour. I'd often go in and out of the center all day, and when "mom" came in it was a big deal. He had two naps, one in the morning and one in the afternoon. When he got a little older and just took one nap, the nap fell right in the middle of the day, so that makes it more difficult. But he knows I'm here and when something happens, like he falls and gets hurt or something, or he gets a cold, they bring him up here, but he doesn't sit there and ask for me."

Marilyn arranged for her husband and herself to be with their infant even when both she and her husband worked fulltime. She says, "I was so lucky I remembered this student intern who had worked for us with children's pal groups, and I contacted her. She was married now and didn't have any children and didn't have a job. I called her up and asked if she would like to take care of Adam. She was delighted, and she was just perfect. She took care of him in her home—it was right on Main Street two blocks from where I worked.

My husband and I went to her house every lunch hour
and I continued to nurse Adam until he was seventeen
months old. My husband worked for the city school
system and both of us were there nearly every day.
Adam was there until he was two and a half and she
moved out of the area, but by then the daycare center
where I worked opened up. The one drawback was
that Adam wasn't with other children. The sitter did
take in a couple of others on a parttime basis, but it
was very temporary. We were the first of our friends to
have kids and, where we lived, we didn't have any contacts with people who had kids, so Adam didn't have
any contacts with other kids till he was two and a half.
I think he would have benefited from other children.
He isn't a very social kid now at five."

Everyone isn't as lucky as Diane and Marilyn. The
choices for infant childcare are very, very limited. The
waiting list is forever in an infant childcare facility. For
example, in the city cited, with a population of 80,000,
there is only *one* group infant-care facility. It's very
possible that you could be offered the greatest career
opportunity in your life, and not be able to get your infant into a center that you felt was good enough. Just
to give you an idea of the problem, according to the
U.S. Senate Finance Committee on Childcare Data,
there are one million "slots" for 6.5 million children of
mothers who are employed fulltime. And most of those
slots or places are not for infants, but for the 3-to-5
year-olds.

If it turns out that you have to work fulltime or even
parttime to support your baby, or if you find out that
you aren't taking sufficiently good care of your baby,
and someone else can do it better, or if you are in an
educational or career situation that keeps you from
caring for your baby all of the time, it may be helpful
for you to know that women who work fulltime think
that their working fulltime is best for their children.
And women who stay home fulltime think that is best.
In other words, people believe in what they are doing,
regardless of what it is. And you will too.

WHAT ARE THE EFFECTS OF INFANT CHILDCARE?

Before you decide what to do about infant care, you will want to ask what happens to infants who are not with their mothers but in a childcare center, or with another caregiver, for a large part of their early life? What will children be like when they grow up, if they start life in a center instead of at home? It will help you to know that regardless of what you hear, *nobody* knows what will happen—in the long run—to group-reared children or to their parents. No studies have been made in the United States of daycare-reared children to see what kinds of adults they have become. And those who have researched childcare have changed their minds as they changed their questions and situations with their own children, and seen more clearly what was going on.

You can't find the answer about how to decide about childcare by understanding the effects of childcare on others, because we just don't know. What you *can* do is look and listen to people who have various caregivers, to learn as much about your baby as you can, to know as much about your own feelings about childcare as you can, and to find out as much as possible about the childcare situations in your area.

CAREGIVERS ARE HUMAN

You may hear that private daycare isn't any good, or that the best place for your child is an employment-sponsored center. As you think about choosing childcare, remember that any kind of childcare—no matter what it is called—is just as good and just as bad as the person who is doing it. Just as any mother is just as good—or just as bad—as the way *she* is doing it. We often talk about childcare as if every baby had a perfect mother, when in fact the mother may put more energy and time into housework than in being with her child. Or she may sit in front of "her" TV programs all day while the child has no one to relate to. Or she may have friends in for coffee all day and never relate to her baby. Or her baby may spend the time with another child most of the day. There are all kinds of ways to be a mother at home with a baby. Mothers of many children are often idealized as if they were giving undivided attention to each of their children. Rare is the mother of many who gives as much as thirty minutes a day of undivided attention to each child. Look around you and ask some such mothers you know how much time alone each child gets. We are really comparing an imperfect childcare situation with an imperfect mother at home. It's the person giving the care who makes the difference—mother or not.

WHAT ARE THE CHILDCARE OPTIONS?

When you get into a situation where you need childcare for your baby, it helps if you already know a little about the possibilities. And because this book is written to help you see things coming, the most common choices for childcare are listed below. When you are ready to look for childcare, you will want to get the most up-to-date costs for the facilities in your area. At that time you can write to the references at the end of this chapter on page 55 ff. You can also look in the yellow pages of the phone book, and check with your local university, hospital, YWCA, churches, and home health agencies. But for an overview, here is what is offered:

YOUR OWN HOME

The expenses of hiring a woman to come to your home vary, from the Certified Home Help Aides who average $2.75 an hour plus transportation, to $1 an hour for a woman who may bring her own young child with her, or who has children in school all day and can be in your home just during school hours. The Certified woman would cost you $123.75 a week, and the woman with children of her own would cost you $40 a week.

A CAREGIVER'S HOME

Probably the cheapest way to get childcare is to take your baby to your mother, cousin, sister, aunt or neighbor. The cost can range from nothing (with some relatives) to $25 to $40 a week. In some cases the young mother may work for six months while a friend cares for the children, then they swap places for the next six months while the other mother goes to work.

FAMILY DAYCARE

More expensive, and most popular, is bringing your baby or children to a woman who takes care of several children in her home. These homes are hard to evaluate, and most of us hear a lot about the bad ones. Some are good. In some cities an agency evaluates these homes and helps you locate them. Look into private home care the same way you would check a center.

DAYCARE CENTERS

Government-sponsored programs are usually attended by welfare children.

Industry-sponsored programs are offered by some companies and businesses, who have their own childcare centers for employees of the company. These are often for low-income families, and the Welfare Department sometimes uses them for getting people off welfare and into work. They are usually open from 7 a.m. to 5 p.m. Most of the costs are paid by welfare. Usually about 10 percent comes from the salaries of the employees.

Cooperative Centers vary. Parents often get together and take turns running a center themselves. Each mother might work one week in two months in the center, which is often located in a church or school setting. The costs average $260 per month for an infant (up to 1-year-old), and $160 for toddlers.

Private run-for-profit centers are chain centers which have sometimes been called Kentucky Friend Children. They are usually open from 7:30 to 5:30 every day, and cost from $45 to $55 a week. Other privately run centers include those owned by businesses which are using the centers for tax shelters. Most are open 50 weeks a year.

University-sponsored centers are established usually for the children of university employees and extended to neighborhood children. The utilities and rent are donated, and the center usually costs about $50 a week. Other similar centers are sponsored by YWCA's, Federal employers, Visiting Nurse's Associations, and Hospital employers.

CHOOSING CHILDCARE: A CHECKLIST

Does this home or center look safe and healthy to you? Are you comfortable with the caregivers' level of housekeeping and cleanliness? A too-clean place can also be a negative indicator. Does it look as though children have fun playing there? Some safety things to look for: Are there sharp objects around? Exposed wiring? Electrical items that could be pulled down? A unprotected fireplace or space heater? Where are household cleansers and medications stored? If you can't see for yourself, don't be afraid to ask:

Does this home (or center) have materials that would interest your child? Think about what your kid(s) like to do at home? Are some of those same things available here?

For babies: Are there bright objects to hold, mouth and play with—hard and soft; noisy and quiet toys? Are there places to crawl, to try pulling up and walking? See how the caregiver feels about playpens; how often are they used? For what length of time? You need not be looking for new, expensive toys. Everyday kitchen objects are wonderful toys and often indicate an imaginative caregiver, smart enough to recognize them as good materials.

For toddlers: Is there room to walk? Are there big things to play with, bean bags, a ball, blocks, a truck or car, a doll? Are there things that come apart or fit inside other things, like shoe boxes, or coffee cans, picture books, a push toy?

Does this caregiver seem like a person you can depend on in an emergency?

Suppose your baby developed a sudden high fever. What if a fire broke out in her home? Could this caregiver administer medication to your child? Would you be able to talk to this person on a regular basis? You will both be involved in your child's day-to-day life, as well as all the routines that go with it (toileting, eating, playing). Practice asking questions now: "What do you feed the children for lunch?" . . . "Where will my child be napping?"

Find out how this person disciplines children. Are you comfortable with the methods she uses? If you do not spank your child, and the caregiver uses spanking as a disciplinary measure, there is a problem! Decide if you want to try to agree on a discipline measure you both like, or look further for another caregiver.

Make sure you get to see the caregiver with children. If your child will be the only one being cared for, watch the caregiver with your child. Here are some things to think about when you are observing:

Does the caregiver look comfortable with kids? Does she smile?

Does she seem interested in them and make eye contact (*even* with newborns)?

Can she comfort children who are hurt or tired?

Can she think of things to interest them or show them?

Does she look like she enjoys taking care of kids?

Do kids who know her look comfortable around her?

Do the kids with her appear to be enjoying each other?

If your child will be transported by the caregiver, ask if she uses seat belts. Provide a car seat if your child is young enough to need one. Does the caregiver carry adequate car insurance?

Will you need to pack your child's lunch or will it be provided? What will be served? Does it sound like a healthy meal to you? Would the caregiver be willing to respect any special diet needs of your child?

What can the caregiver expect of you? Make certain you can be reached by telephone during the day. Have a good "back-up" person (relative or friend) for when you are not at your work-site.

Let your pediatrician know who your caregiver is.

Unless you have worked out special arrangements with your caregiver, don't bring your child to her if the child is sick.

Provide the things that your child will need to wear—diapers, a change of clothes, vaseline.

Pay your bills promptly; if you receive public funding for childcare, keep your certificate up to date.

Remember—and you know this as a parent: Taking care of children *well* requires a lot of energy. Let your caregiver know that you appreciate that.

The way to enjoy your work or school situation is to be sure your baby is safe and in a growing environment when you are not there. It's important for both you and your husband to be both comfortable and well informed.

When you first put your baby into another caregiver's hands, keep in mind that it often takes children some time—maybe even a couple of months—to become comfortable in a new environment. Just think about how long it takes you to get used to a new job, or neighborhood, or school. If you need to work or go to school, and you trust the childcare arrangements you have made, stick with them. Look for signs that your child is becoming more at ease. Make certain that the caregiving facilities are inadequate before deciding to change.

Because you need a support system for all new situations, discuss what is happening with your friends. Talk with other parents whose judgment you trust and who are having similar experiences. That way, you can help each other find and choose a good caregiver, and continue to share notes about being working parents or student parents. Invest some thought and planning in a place for your baby before you put your baby there. Then watch closely for your baby's reaction while settling in. If you exercise these precautions you will be able to relax and trust your judgment because you did plan carefully.

CHILDCARE AGENCIES AND INFORMATION CENTERS

Write for more about childcare to:

Association for Childhood International
3615 Wisconsin Avenue N.W.
Washington, D.C. 20016

Black Child Development Institute
1028 Connecticut Avenue N.W.
Washington, D.C. 20036

Child Development Consortium
7315 Wisconsin Avenue
Washington, D.C. 20014

Child Study Association of America
School of Social Work
New York University
New York, N.Y. 12206

Child Welfare League of America, Inc.
67 Irving Place
New York, N.Y. 10003

Day Care and Child Development
Council of America, Inc.
1012 Fourteenth Street N.W.
Washington, D.C. 20005

Department of Labor
Women's Bureau
Constitution Avenue and Fourteenth Street N.W.
Washington, D.C. 20210

National Association for the
Education of Young Children
1834 Connecticut Avenue N.W.
Washington, D.C. 20009

Office of Child Development
U.S. Dept. of Health, Education and Welfare
Washington, D.C. 20201

"IT'S A BABY!"

We have all heard that babies need love. We haven't all heard exactly what that means. Infants, for example, would prefer that you hold them close, talk to them, play with them and give them your undivided attention over hearing about that "special warm feeling" adults get when they see a baby. In other words, babies would prefer that you know more about child development than you know about love and romance.

We have all heard that children grow and change. We haven't all heard that, because of children, parents and adults grow and change too.

We have all heard about the excitement of couples expecting their first baby. We've heard much less about the 8 million single mothers who have to go it alone.

"It's a baby!" can be good news for any woman. Learning about children's needs, learning what to expect from a baby, learning to sharpen your observation and responsive skills toward another human being can help you—regardless of your situation—to enjoy your baby.

"It's a baby!" can be your baby's good news.

LOVE IS MORE
THAN A FEELING

by the Reverend
Patricia Budd Kepler

Religion is about relationship to God. Religion also is about the way we relate to each other. Religion has to do with love and love is more than a feeling. It is a way of acting toward another person. The most important love relationships we have, most important because they are most formative, the most intense, long-term, are relationships in families. And love in families is very complex. You have probably noticed that. Up until now you have been mostly concerned with being a daughter. Now as you read this book you are thinking about being a mother.

Becoming a mother is relatively easy for most women. Being a mother is not easy. Being a loving person is not something we can do automatically. It is something we have to learn how to do.

We hear mothers and fathers say they love their children. We know that they do. Then we see or hear about or experience those same parents treating their children in ways that don't seem very loving at all. What happens?

People want to love, but sometimes they just don't know how to. Parents have learned patterns of interacting from their own parents. They have needs to be fulfilled. They are told by society to expect certain things

59

from each other. There is a difference between wanting to love, feeling love for another person, and being able to act out love. Acting out love means doing what is best for the other person and for yourself in a real two-way encounter.

Religion, God, Faith, is expressed and experienced in *acting out love.* What is *acting out* love between parent and child like? First of all, love always means acknowledging the other human being as a person who is not to be used primarily to meet your needs. In a recent survey of teenage mothers it was found that they had babies to have someone all to themselves. Someone to love them. They were feeling very lonely. They were feeling unloved. Their babies were supposed to fill their emptiness. That is not love. That is *needing love.* We are not ready to be parents until we are ready to *give love.* A child is not to fill our empty places. A child is someone with whom to share our fullness. Of course our own needs will come out in our relationship with our children, but we must be in control of them. We need to *get ourselves together first,* before we are good parents. Becoming a parent is not a way to get oneself together. A child cannot be used.

Secondly a child is not a possession to be owned, like a car or a doll, or an animal. A baby is a sacred human being, a tiny developing life. It is a parent's responsibility to cherish that special life and respect it. A baby is not just an extension of oneself; a baby is a separate, individual life, even if in her early years she is dependent on you. Love means acting that out. Being ready to help someone else grow up. Of course it is hard to do that if you are not ready to be mature yourself. It is hard to let another person be herself or himself if you do not feel free to be yourself. Women sometimes are taught to live their lives through other people. When they do they may begin to treat other people as if they belong to them. A child becomes a mother's reason for being. You need to know who you are so you won't try to become someone through your baby.

On the other hand, both a mother and a father have to be willing to give up some of their time and energy for a baby. They have to be ready to pay attention to their child. Another thing about love is that it takes time and energy. Sometimes men learn that they don't have to give up much energy or time for a baby. Being a parent is mostly a mother's job. Before you are married you need to talk about this with the person you love. Each couple needs to work out their own lifestyle. But however you work it out, a child needs time and attention from both a mother and a father. You may have grown up in a family with one parent. Single-parent families can be very loving. But being a single parent is not easy—both mothers and fathers have been courageous and strong in their single-parenting. Sometimes events in life interrupt the mother-father parenting. But you will be beginning at the beginning. A man will father your child. Both of you need to be willing to take responsibility and devote time to loving. Loving takes time and energy.

Loving takes understanding and wisdom. When you have a child you must be prepared to teach your child how to be safe, how to survive, how to get along with other people, how to make moral judgments, how to think for himself. Loving means giving direction. It means sometimes being able to say "no" with firmness. It means being a teacher. It means setting an example. It means being clear yourself about what is right and wrong and not living by a double standard—that is, doing one thing and telling your child to do another.

Love means hanging in with the other person even when the going is rough. Being a parent is a long-term commitment. It is not a brief satisfaction. There will be difficult times. Times when children are sick, or tired, or going through a difficult stage, or testing limits. A mother must hang in through all of these times. It is important to think about these kinds of times before having a baby. There is no point in living with an illusion of an always-happy bundle of joy. We need to be prepared for hard times. If we are, we will always be able to handle them.

Love does not mean losing one's life in the other. Women today are discovering that with planning, and preparation, and working things through with partners, they can be mothers and also pursue those things that are important to them in their own lives. Love takes time and energy. But it does not mean total sacrifice. We need to bring our whole selves into love relationships and stand as complete people. Our children need to respect us. They need to see that we care about society and are willing to put energy into making it better. They need to know that we have friends and are not totally dependent on them. They need to learn about friendship from seeing us with other people. They need to learn to share us.

Love is forgiving and asking for forgiveness. No matter how hard we try to respect the other person and ourselves, we sometimes fail. No one is perfect all the time. As mothers we will often have to say we are sorry. We will sometimes have to be able to say we are hurt or angry. We can't forgive unless we are up front with our feelings. We need to learn to express our feelings with our children and teach them to express theirs. We can't express our feelings if we don't know ourselves—if we are out of touch with how we feel.

Love means being changed by the other person. If we are open to one another we will be so affected by the other person that that person will change us. Our children are bound to have a profound influence on us if we let them. We obviously will have a profound influence on them. It needs to be a two-way street. Parents have many years on children. They have been formed over a long period of time. Parents also are faced with the awesome task of teaching children and giving them guidance. It is hard to stand one's own ground and still be open to change. But it can be done. We can be sensitive to the fact that the life in our care is unique. We can be sensitive to the fact that the world our children experience is in some very important ways different from the world in which we lived. Of course there are some values which transcend time, and our age and experience gives us insight not available to the inexperienced. Yet, there is something to be learned from our children. They are experiencing the world in fresh ways. They see things in us that we may be blind to or have chosen to ignore. They may not so easily accept the compromises with which we have made our peace. They may not know how costly they have been, and we have forgotten. The point about children is that the world changes and they come to it with fresh eyes. In any human interaction which is alive and dynamic, people are going to affect each other. We must be prepared to give, to be flexible, to change. Allowing another to so deeply affect our lives is part of love.

You are a young woman who can choose when and if to become a mother. That decision will be one of the most important you will make in your life. It must not be taken lightly. When you are thinking about it, you can think about some of these things. Being a Christian or a Jew means respecting life as sacred.

It means acting out the love of God in human relationships.

I am a mother and a minister. My own sons are teenagers now. I have learned these things about love from them. I have struggled with being my own person, working, doing what is important to me and being a mother to them. My husband and I have struggled with our joint responsibilities for parenting. We have both done "mothering" and "fathering" things. Sometimes it has been very hard to work out, but remembering that love is hard work has helped. Love is what life is all about. It is a source of joy and strength. It is its own reward. You can prepare for motherhood. You can learn to know yourself. You can share in your family. You can learn to express your feelings, to be sensitive to others expressing their feelings. You can learn to hang into relationships when the going gets tough. You can find out what you want to do in school and work, and program yourself to do it. You can grow.

And you can learn from your own parents. You can take advantage of being a daughter. Think about how you feel your experience as a daughter. You can try to find ways to talk with your mother about her own mother. You can learn about your past and try to understand why your own parents feel and act the way they do. You can try to imagine their side, and that may help to set you free to be the kind of person and parent you want to be.

Acting out love in our human encounters is a gift of life. Being in relationship with my family and with other people returns me to God. Sometimes I need to be alone, to be by myself, to find a source of strength and courage from deep inside myself and from God, so that I can gain a perspective on life and relationship. If I did not have God to turn to, I would be in danger of making idols out of the people I love. That is, I would be in danger of making them be all things to me. I would not be able to ever let go. I would not be able to stand alongside of other people and face them. I would cling to them, enter into them, have trouble sorting out who I am from who they are. That would be destructive of others and of myself. My relationship to God and to people keeps life in balance. One without the other creates all kinds of problems in life. If I use my relationship with God to run away from the very people I have given to love, God cannot speak to me through those who are also God's people. I cannot learn to grow in depth. I cannot fully experience life. If on the other hand I live only through relationships with people and hide from God, I cannot really learn about myself and the ultimate meaning of existence. I idolize the world and people.

Motherhood requires closeness and distance. There are times to touch and hold very close. And there are times to let go and step aside. There are times to turn to God and times to turn to one another. There are times to be in relationship with others and times to be in relationship to ourselves and to God. It is a gift of the created order that life is arranged so that when we live in these three ways the blessings of life unfold before us. When we deny any one of them life becomes stagnant and frightening. Motherhood is a gift. Being in such close relationship with another human being is part of the great mystery and joy of life. Being in relationship with God and in touch with ourselves is another gift. It too is part of the great mystery and joy of life. The real surprise is how intimately all the strands of our life are interconnected.

A HALF-DAY WITH 8-MONTH-OLD KATE

by the father of Kate,
Larry Daloz

I'm lucky this morning. I get past Kate's crib without waking her. If she wakes now I've had it—me half dressed, her, the fire, and my growling stomach all demanding to be stoked at once. Once I'm in the kitchen, pulling on my pants as I go, I can get the fire going and maybe even have something to eat before her wail goes off.

No such luck. I'm just loading the stove, arms full of wood, when it comes, welcome as an alarm clock. I go in, try in vain to stuff the pacifier into her protesting mouth and then, realizing the hopelessness of it all, manage a hypocritical smile. "Good morning, Kate." In my arms her crying changes almost at once to gentle cooing. My stomach drops and I hug her. She nuzzles sleepily into my shoulder. I'm helpless.

After a quick diaper change it's time for breakfast. Into the highchair she goes bellowing. Quickly, I mix a cupful of cottage cheese and applesauce and slip it into her mouth between complaints. The first few spoonfuls go well until she decides to help herself. Her hand and the spoon play keep-away for a moment or two until she wins. In no time her face is a riot of cottage cheese. But gradually she grows less insistent, gazing for longer periods into the distance. "All through?" I ask. Seeing no response I decide for her and, wetting a cloth, begin to restore her face to its original innocence. Violent protest. Howls. Squirms. I grit my teeth, saying with millions of parents before me what I hated to be told, "It's for your own good, kid."

We then retire with bottle to watch the morning news. President Carter has the nomination. Kate sucks intensely on the nipple. Interest rates are up to 20%. Kate drops the bottle and arches her back, looking at the world upside down. Finally, as we learn of the latest oil prices, Kate has had enough. I set her on the floor and, like a wind-up toy, she's off, headed for a particularly fascinating cluster of ball, magazine and truck about three feet off. At last I have a moment to sip my coffee and hear Joe DiMaggio tell me how much better off I'd be if I only bought Mr. Coffee from him. No sooner have I politely declined, than Kate is back at my feet. She pulls herself up and wants to cuddle. I oblige and we are soon having a tickling match on the rug. Giggles. Then a squirm and it's time to finish the bottle.

But the bottle doesn't seem to satisfy her. She begins to whine again so I check her. Sure enough, it's time for a change. While we are getting fresh water in the bathroom, she grins at us both in the mirror. Almost as if to check which is real, she looks up at me, then back, greeting herself this time with a squeal of delight. While we're changing, I sing her "Tea for Two": Da daddee, Da daddaa. She smiles back and murmurs to herself: Da da da da. Fortunately the mess was small this time and we're soon freshly packaged.

About now I'm beginning to wonder if I'll ever eat again. I decide to put her in the playpen—affectionately labeled "the cage." Will it work? Miraculously, it does. She becomes absorbed in her rattle and Mr. Jimmy's big Georgia smile. I tiptoe away, leaving her contentedly beating him over the head with a doll.

Stove restoked, I finally put together a quick breakfast before she has had enough of the cage. Captain Kangaroo has taken over by now and Kate is beginning to show signs of naptime. I hold her for a few minutes and her eyes gradually begin to glaze. Yawn. Rock her gently. Eyelids drop, and I quietly lay her in the crib. Pacifier in place. Sleep!

The break gives me a chance to do the breakfast dishes—quietly, quietly!—and I have a moment to catch up on my reading. How long it will be is anyone's guess. At her present 8-month age, we can usually count on at least a half-hour; sometimes as long as two hours, though this is almost inevitably at the cost of a good afternoon nap.

This morning we make it for about 45 minutes. Then I see her begin to toss, a grunt, a miniature pant, a snort, and, like a tiny locomotive she puffs back to life. Pulling herself to her feet, she beams at me. Sheer delight. The sun is streaming through the window and I beam back, restraining myself from going over and giving her a hug. But she's in a good mood and I decide to let her enjoy it without interference. I slip out of the room and prepare her mid-morning juice.

By the time it's ready, she has had enough of the crib and calls out to me. I answer, she smiles, and I shake my head. More beams. Chuckles. I make a Bronx cheer. She does the same, then giggles. We converse this way for a while between giggles. All at once her exuberance overwhelms her and she tips over backwards. Righting herself, her attention is taken by a mobile near the wall. She talks to it for a moment, then rediscovers me and her face contorts. She wants out.

With a hug, I whisk her off for a change. Her high spirits present something of a problem. She squirms and kicks and giggles, trying to reach the bowl of rinse water. I manage to wrestle off a bootie and hand it to her. This distracts her sufficiently while I pull off the soaked diaper and wipe her off with warm water. She's all dried off and I'm just reaching for the salve to sooth a touch of rash when it happens. Frantically, I try to tear off a piece of paper towel with my free hand while I hold her with the other. The roll pitches and bobs, refusing to oblige. By the time I finally succeed, it's too late. Nothing remains undampened but her enthusiasm. The scrap of towel arrives in time to dab up the last dribble from her little orifice.

I groan, lecture myself on the innocence of babies,

take a deep breath, and begin unwrapping her. Everything has to come off. Sweater, overalls, stretch suit. Fortunately her undershirt is still OK. Naturally, the whole event is enormous fun for Kate, who squeals and gurgles her way through the lengthy mop-up operation. I don't quite see it that way.

Back in the living room, she makes short work of her apple juice and is off exploring. Keeping one eye on her, I sit at the desk writing checks, paying bills. It goes well. A stack of records absorbs her attention for quite a while before she decides to climb up on them and reach for the top of a neighboring chest. She's such a great climber that I can't resist letting her practice. I kneel beside her and encourage her as she laboriously hoists her knee onto the top of the chest. She struggles this way for a while and finally, with a little help, finds a foothold for the other foot. By this time she is two feet off the floor, so I stay close, ready to catch her as she peers uncertainly over the precipice. Then, having let her savor the prize, I put her gently back onto the floor, aim her toward the low window and return to my work. She drinks in the winter scenery, beating delightedly on the window for some time before peeling off toward the legs of the crib to initiate an intensive study of the casters.

For an hour the tour goes on as I watch, alternately participating and observing as the situation demands. She makes her way around the room in a ragged orbit, punctuated by exploratory stops and short-circuits to me for reassurance.

Once, pulling herself up on a table leg, she loses her balance and goes over backwards. In that suspended moment before she decides what has happened, I am beside her, reassuring. "You're OK, Kate. Here . . ." I extend a finger for her to grasp. She pulls herself up. No tears. She tries again and this time succeeds.

Another time, she swings by the stove. She reaches out tentatively. "No, Kate. It's hot!" She stops, looks back over her shoulder. Questions. I look stern. "Hot!" Hands drop hesitantly to her side. Then slowly, on to the other side of the room. We find a ball and play with it. I retire. She continues. Later, her itinerary leads again toward the stove. Again, "No, Kate, hot!" and this time, with a glance in my direction, she steers clear, cruising past toward an inviting magazine. The magazine is reduced to shreds, a bit of cloth wags aimlessly, and she's cruising again.

In the meantime, I take her lunch out of the freezer and set it on the stove to thaw. Beets. Green beans. Chicken. I change her diapers and plunk her in the highchair. This sets off a frenzy of dissatisfaction. Patience is clearly not one of her virtues. A bit of cheese quiets her while I make myself a quick sandwich and stir the thawing vegetables.

She eats sporadically, obviously tired and ready for sleep. This causes her to rub her eyes with fingers fresh from a mouthful of beets. Red eyes. Something in her ear itches. Green ears. But eventually we got more on the inside than out, and as I'm about to wipe her face off, the telltale grimace appears. She grunts and pants alternately until her business is done and she sits, glassy-eyed with exhaustion. I weather the storm of protest while I wipe her face and then whisk her off to be changed. Naturally, the sitting position has spread her recent effort far and wide, so it is some time before I finally get her freshly wrapped. But the effort has also exhausted her, and before long she's sound asleep. Peace at last. It is noon.

꧁ • ꧂

ACTION

Playtime is love time. Playing with your child is the action of TLC (tender loving care). TLC is something you do *for* a baby. Action is something you do *with* baby. When you care for a baby, your baby feels dependent. When you play with a baby, you can teach him to see skills he has learned so that he will begin to feel some control and independence—even at 6-months.

Some parents don't realize how important undivided attention is to the growth of their children. If parents fail to interrelate with their children or wait for some other adult who is crazy about the children to perform this parental function for them, the children become stressful and unhappy, often expressing it by constantly acting out. Then, after months or years of no special times, you will have to put in a lot more time to make up for the hurt feelings and nonspecial feelings the child has acquired. Every child needs the interaction of playing with parents.

Playtime is love time as far as your baby is concerned. Help your baby learn the skills that will lead to a feeling of achievement and control. Start building those special playtimes with your baby the first week of the baby's life. It's fun. It's basic. You'll both thrive.

"There's nothing to do!"
"Can I watch TV, Mommy?"
"What can I do today?"
When your child looks to you for something to do, say:

"Let's . . . read a book
make up a story
play a record
write a poem
make music
put on a play
make puppets
go to the zoo
toss the beanbag
roll the ball
play cards
go for a tricycle ride
go to the art gallery
go to the natural-history museum
make a present
write a birthday card
make Christmas wrapping paper
color Easter eggs
have an Easter egg hunt
pick a bouquet of flowers
wash the car
wash the windows
pop popcorn
make play-dough
paint a picture
paint a room
paint the house
plant an herb garden
bake bread
walk the dog
brush the dog
mop the floor
vacuum the rug
sweep the porch
unpack the groceries
polish the silver
polish shoes
fold the laundry
rake the yard
polish furniture
take a night walk
look at the stars

    go to the library
    go to a band concert
    visit the firehouse
    dig for worms
    play on the jungle gym
    play in the park
    backpack in the park
    bake cookies
    make a pudding
    climb a ladder
    hammer nails into the ground
    push a wheelbarrow
    go on a picnic
    go sliding
    go rock hunting
    go berry picking
    go wildflower tripping
    go swimming
    go fishing
    make a costume
    make-up a face
    make Christmas tree decorations
    make Christmas and birthday gifts
    make up a holiday to celebrate
    draw a picture
    finger paint
    paste a picture
    plant a garden
    start a houseplant
    start a plant from an avocado seed!"

This list will get you started on the great variety of activities found right at home or close by. Even everyday activities become very special when you plan them with your child. Making music can consist of hitting a pot with a wooden spoon to the tune of a child's record or the radio. Or blowing on wax paper folded over a comb. Making puppets or a mask can consist of painting a paper bag, or coloring a sock or paper bag for use as a hand puppet or a mask for over the head, or making-up a face with your own makeup (using cold cream, first, of course!). You can make big cards for a 2-year-old—the child can color them and you can cut them out. You can also make up your own card game.

A visit to the fire station or art gallery might be fun. Or a visit to the natural-history museum in a stroller to see the stuffed bears—and for a very short time (say 10 or 15 minutes in the building).

Drawing with markers on tissue paper for holiday or special birthday wrapping paper can begin at a very young age. Painting with washable latex paint can start just before 3. Walking and brushing the dog, plus putting the food and water out for the pets, can start around 2—a little earlier for some children. Helping to put away the groceries is an activity for an 18-month-old (for *some* groceries, but not the eggs).

A very exciting backpack or tricycle trip can be arranged with many special sessions to plan, arrange and pack for the trip. A small backpack containing raisins, an orange, carrot sticks and other precious possessions can be just what a 2-year-old prizes most. A trip to the park or up a grassy hill in the back yard will be a very special event when planned that way. In snow country, sliding and building snow-people, igloos and forts are special activities which can be started as soon as the children can walk, as long as your child is dressed warmly enough. And, in beach country, playing in the water and sand can begin at an early age too. (Protection from the sun is needed along with a careful eye on your baby's face while playing in the water.) Preparing a garden spot, and having the child drop in the seeds and cover them up, is an activity they can enjoy both then and later, as they watch the seedlings grow and care for the plants by weeding or watering in future weeks. But the under-3's need lots of help; these beginners can't be expected to grow a garden or tend houseplants on their own. Picking berries and wildflowers is also fun. The berries and flowers can be put in something special and given away—your child's gift to someone else.

Children's activities can grow into gifts and giving. The time you give to your child now provides a way they can learn to give of themselves and their possessions later, when they are teenagers and then parents. The time you are giving to your child now develops your own creative and persuasion skills—as well as concentration and persistence.

LEARNING SKILLS

An action or an adventure is a special time with your baby. Learning skills through work and play, through arts and crafts, and helping with the basic family needs, are actions which make children feel good. These special times make babies and little children feel more confident and loved, more *in* on life, and less of a tag-along. It makes them respected, independent—even at the age of 1—and able. To a child, there's not much difference between work and play. In many ways you will come to realize that play is the child's work. Learning skills and everything his body can do is the job of your child. You are helping him to learn and to feel good about his accomplishments, whether it's putting pressure against your hand as you push his 3-months'-old foot as he lays on his back, or tossing beanbags into a big cardboard box. Such physical energy develops balance, eye-hand coordination, and other things a child needs to feel in control. Skills are empowering. As you begin to see that it's not what you do for your children that builds respect for themselves, but *what they can learn to do for themselves*, you will understand the importance of helping them to learn skills on their own. Skills—even at 6 months— teach the baby that she really does have some control over her body and life—and that she can take some responsibility for it.

A SPECIAL TIME

If you start a special playtime with your baby—even when he is only a week old, you will get in the habit of enjoying each other on a regular basis, and learning from each other. During the first few weeks, just five minutes of uninterrupted playtime, or cuddling time, out of every half-hour or hour he is awake (in addition to when he is getting fed or bathed) will be very special times for both of you.

Don't rush the activity when the baby gets a little older and you decide to take a five- or ten-minute time with her. It doesn't really matter how much she gets done, or learned, or how many pictures she gets colored, or seeds planted, or leaves raked. If the baby is always rushed, as parents often are, they will always feel under stress, and that isn't the fun idea you started with at all! After you make the decision that you are going to give your baby five or ten minutes of your uninterrupted time—no TV, no radio, no phone calls, just you and your baby—then relax and let the time and play go as it will. Nothing can be more important than for your child to learn that this is *his* time with you, with no other set goals, with nothing specific that your child *has* to learn in that time. You enjoy this time solely because it is your time with your baby.

TV TIME

TV is *not* a special time for infants and early toddlers. TV may be a special time for parents—special only because you pacify your baby or toddler with television in order to get some time alone. But getting some time alone by turning on the TV for your baby may not be worth it, because all the evidence shows that TV dims the young mind, and all that passivity is habit-forming.

With too much TV, regardless of the quality of the programs, there is no way your little baby can grow up to be a fully active human being. A child needs to experience plenty of interaction within his family in order to grow up with the skills necessary for good relationships. It's hard to say "no" to toddlers at any time, but it's even harder the later you start. Children have their own ways to get what they want, and it's easy to feel sorry for them when they "don't have anything to do." But not until they *know* they can't watch television (and that may take from ten to thirty minutes of hassling), will they turn their thoughts to a creative idea, a game, a book, a bike ride, a walk, a slide in the snow, cooking, cleaning their room, writing a skit, putting on makeup and all the other things they will come up with, if you create a home environment which encourages them to be creative with their time.

A CREATIVE ENVIRONMENT

When Margaret Mead was a little girl her mother didn't just tell her to "go play." Instead, she told her to go and listen to all the different sounds her baby brother was making. As young Margaret got a little older (around 5), she was told to notice how many words he could say. One of the most observing anthropologists in the world began to learn those observation skills right at home—watching the development of her baby brother.

Observation skills are important in your career development because so much of the information you gather about the world depends on what you can see and hear. When applied to other peoples' behavior, observation skills help you to see details, to notice differences and to be sensitive to how people act. These skills add to your personal enjoyment of life as well as to your career development. They provide an ability to tune-in to others.

One good place to start observing others is to look at your younger brothers and sisters, or neighbors, or cousins, and their physical and social development. Young children change so rapidly that you have to notice all kinds of actions to get a true and accurate indication of their age. If you babysit with babies or toddlers, or if you just watch them at play, or ask a mother questions about their development, you will learn a lot about the differences in development between children. You will also notice the many things babies at 3 months, or 6, or 9 have in common.

It's amazing to learn that three-quarters or more of all children (American, and in good health) will probably do much the same things at much the same ages. When relatives get all excited about a baby's development, it sounds like this: "Does he turn over yet?" Does he sit up?" "Does he wave bye-bye?" For the most part, they can depend on the fact that the baby will turn over at 5 months, sit up at 6 months and wave bye-bye at 10 months! In other words, you can usually get the clues to the baby's age—even when the baby's size is smaller or larger than average—from his behavior.

OBSERVATION ACTIVITIES

Here are some activities that are fun to watch for with a young baby up to two years old. These typical behavior patterns were determined by Harvard professor Dr. Burton L. White, who researched early childhood for seventeen years before writing *The First Three Years of Life*. Dr. White points out that the age given is the age when you can expect the baby to *begin* the particular behavior. For example, the children will start to climb a stair at from 7 to 11 months, the average being 9 months. In other words, the process of climbing a stair can start from 7 to 11 months, although most babies start at 9.

Action! Physical and Social	Age in months when babies start this action
Holds head steady while in an upright position	2 to 4 - 3
Turns over from front to back, back to front	4 to 6 - 5
Reaches for an object	4 to 7 - 5
Sits up alone	5 to 8 - 6
Crawls or scoots	6 to 12 - 8
Climbs a stair	7 to 11 - 9
Climbs an object a foot high	8 to 14 - 11
Climbs down stairs	10 to 15 - 11
Walks while holding on to furniture	9 to 15 - 11
Walks alone	9 to 16 - 12
Rides a four-wheel toy	14 to 20 - 16
Startles to sharp noises	birth to 3 months
Gums the fists	birth to 2
Looks at own hands and	

faces of others	2 to 4
Sucks and gums any object	2 to 4
Bats with hands	2 to 4
Socializes and smiles	2 to 4
Notices mother or primary caregiver	4 to 5
Looks around	4 to 5
Hand-eye activities such as batting, reaching and grasping	4 to 5
Turns over	4 to 5
Makes and listens to own sounds	4 to 5
Simple hand activities with small objects	5 to 8
Practice in sitting up	5 to 8
Notices words, listens to own sounds	5 to 8
Stays awake for several hours	1½ to 2½ - 2
First simple ability to control hands	1½ to 2½ - 2
Controls head	2 to 4 - 3
Unclenches fingers	2 to 4 - 3
Has head control when sitting up	3 to 5 - 4
Turns body to the side	4 to 5 - 4
Turns over	5
Reaches for objects	5
Understands words	7 to 10 - 8
Sees everything	7 to 11 - 9
Understands several dozen words	9 to 16 - 12
Waves bye-bye	9 to 12 - 10
Speaks first words	12 to 24 - 13

Copy this list and, when you are with a baby, check off the activities as you can see the baby perform them. Find out the exact age of the baby and note which of these activities the baby does all of the time, or sometimes. After you have made your observations, check them out with the average age for child development on the list.

How did you do? Could you see the baby doing many of these activities? What did her mother say about the baby's development? After several observation practices, you might want to observe the baby *before* you find out her age, then guess her age by your observations. Check with the baby's mother to see how well you guessed.

Knowing about child development will help you in problem-solving when you are a mother. You will learn to plan fun and play activities with your baby depending on her development. And what you learn now will be a good foundation for understanding your baby later. It's fun to watch babies grow.

EVERY DAY
WITH TLC

Often a new baby isn't as enthusiastic about life in her new world as she was about the warm and dark womb where she was being comforted by the regular heartbeat sounds of her mother's heart. A baby has to learn what's it like to be with people, even his mother, before he decides that life is okay. It's not just getting the proper food into the baby, keeping her dry and burping up the gas so that she can sleep well. That's not all the baby needs. It's *how* all of these things are done that teaches the baby what living in the world with other human beings is like. If the nipple of the breast or bottle is offered gently and as often as wanted, and the baby is held very close, he can learn to trust the firmness, closeness and presence of others. If, on the other hand, the baby has to raise the roof to get anyone present to feed her, burp her, change her, hold her, she will learn another way to view the world. Besides learning the what and when to give the baby, a new mother, then, must also develop a sense of *how* to care for her baby. A mother must develop a sense of what she is teaching her baby about life with people. A sense of closeness between mother and baby is the beginning of that learning. Helping your baby to feel OK in this new world is the crucial task of the new mother.

BABY AND MAMA KNOW BEST

Right from the start—when you are still carrying him—you and your baby become a team. His presence influences how you feel and what you do, and your presence does the same for the baby. Building a working team with your baby starts when you tune in to where your baby is, how she feels, what she is like, being sensitive to her unique personality. Sometimes we get the idea that babies are born without their own personalities and that we can mold them any way we want to. But after they arrive, it doesn't take long to catch on that babies do have their own needs, their own growth patterns, their own energy levels.

A good working team develops when you each learn to respect the uniqueness of the other. It's exciting to build a relationship with a baby. And it's also scary. What if you don't observe the right clues? What if you don't do the right thing? What if you thought the crying was because he had too much to eat and the real problem was that he didn't have enough? Luckily for all mothers, babies thrive even when their mothers aren't always right. Babies thrive in spite of the many misjudgments of a new mother. They thrive as their parents are learning to pick up the clues that help make a good working team. How will you learn to tune in with your baby?

There are hundreds of books about baby care—and you will probably want to look at some of them, and own one that you can keep within close reach. Most of the baby books are written by white male "experts" in child care and development, such as Spock, Salk and Caplan. Mothers tend to listen to the so-called experts as if they knew exactly what to do and had all the answers. But just like experts in any field, if you read many of them, you will see that one expert says one thing and another says something else. Just as with clothes, fads and fashions come and go in baby care. Breast feeding or bottle feeding; demand feeding versus schedules; solids early or solids late; eggs early, no eggs, or eggs late; let the baby cry, pick the baby up immediately, let the baby cry a little while; use baby powder, use baby oil, or don't use either powder or oil; pat the baby gently on the back or don't pat but rub in a circular motion to get up the burp. Use a pacifier, don't use a pacifier.

If you read and listen to all the views written, you'll be a wreck trying to decide what to do with your first baby! Of course it's good to read the experts for general ideas. And of course you will want to ask your pediatrician for her views. But even though it's your first baby, you may be surprised at how quickly you can learn to notice and observe and really begin to know when feeding, rocking, cuddling, comforting, changing, playing and sleeping are just right for your baby. You will soon learn to have confidence in what you see and what you hear. *Your baby will give you all kinds of clues about his happy or unhappy states.* It will soon be a matter of trying two or three things, till you come up with the right thing to stop the crying. Problem-solving is one of the mothering skills that soon will be yours.

TRUST YOURSELF

How can you know, how can you decide what to do if you don't listen to the experts? It takes time to learn, and practice to trust yourself, to trust what you see and hear and feel. It takes time to trust the observation skills you are learning, to trust your experience with your baby.

Start with yourself. There is no one in the world who knows you yourself as well as you do. Pay attention to your physical and emotional needs—your sleeping and eating and moving and action needs. Notice when you need some sleep or a snack; notice when you are patient and when you are impatient. Notice the yelling you do, the crying, and laughing. When do you do these things? Try getting to know yourself as your baby knows you.

TRUST YOUR BABY

Just as you can learn how you feel and what you need, you can learn also that there is no other person in the world (even an expert) who knows your baby as well as you do. Notice when your baby laughs, cries, needs your undivided attention, can't be kept happy, needs to eat. To sleep. To play. Needs *you*. With a tiny infant, it's a matter of noticing the baby's body language—her eyes, her arms up wanting to come to mama, her voice, her smiles, her tears. If you are the primary person in your baby's life, you will get to know your baby so much better than a doctor, or grandmother, or daycare or social worker, that there isn't anyone else who can give you better information about your baby than you yourself!

It's because you are the expert that your baby needs you until he can trust other people for his needs. It's because you will come when you are needed, or leave him alone when everything is OK, that is crucial for the baby to have you—or your advice and observations—for his caregiver until he is 2. If someone else takes care of him most of the day, you will want to share what you know about your baby in detail with that caregiver.

Your baby is also learning to trust her own feelings as you respond to her. If you have an allergic baby or child, for example, chances are that it won't be long before the child feels the wheezing or rash coming on—even before you see and hear it. The child, then, becomes the expert about her own body—just as you are the expert about your body, about how you feel and what you need.

TRUST OTHERS

All of this may sound as if you shouldn't take *any* advice. Sure, take it! Listen to tons of it. But make it your own by relating it to your situation and your baby's life *before* you try it out. Don't be afraid to change the advice a little bit. Or change it a lot. Come up with something that may vary a little and really work best for you. If you know that you can change advice to meet your needs, you won't mind getting it. Lots of people like to give advice to new mothers. There are lots of times when you will want to ask for advice, especially from someone who has a child or two, and has already been through exactly what you are worried about. It feels good to ask for advice when you know you can sift through it according to what you know works in your family, and makes sense to you and your child.

EXPECT CHANGE

Childcare is one constant change, trying things out and making alternative plans. One week it works well to give the baby an hour's nap in the morning. The next week it works better for two hours. Then three months later, the baby has changed again and none of that works. As the expert in charge of this baby, don't get stuck in what you did last week. Keep looking for the change in reaction, for the sense of thriving and feeling that tells you it's working real good now. What works well now, you will soon know, will not necessarily work later. If you *expect* change in how you go about your baby's daily care, it will be a fascinating—rather than a frustrating—experience for you. It's the changes that bring growth. It's the challenge of figuring it all out that keeps childcare so interesting. That's where you learn flexibility, problem-solving and time-management skills.

FEEDING

There is no end to the research that has been done to show that babies desperately need physical contact, tender loving care and as much hugging and cuddling as they can get during their first few months. As milk builds the baby's physical health, touching and physical closeness while the baby is being fed builds her emotional and mental health. When you begin to realize the time you will be putting into feeding a new baby, then you begin to realize, too, how much it counts. You will want to be prepared to feed your baby in the warmest, closest way possible.

Breast feeding is the easiest way to feed a new baby. No formula, no nipples to sterilize, no stuff to carry around, no refrigeration and no heating the milk. Another advantage of breast feeding is that the baby gets a lot more sucking—which they all need—with less milk than she can with a bottle. I think that if new babies could vote on what they prefer, they would all vote to be breast fed! It must feel good to the baby in close to his mother, to have his face against his mother's breast, to have the undivided attention of his mother for that part of the day when he is eating (which can be up to 8 times a day, 40 minutes a time—which is about 5½ hours every single day for the first few months!).

If breast feeding is ideal for you and your baby, then it makes sense to do it. If you decide for any reasons not to breast feed (you are anxious about it, you aren't going to be home with the baby, her father is going to share in the feeding, you don't like the Mother Nature feeling of breast feeding, you can't seem to relax enough to enjoy it, you don't have enough milk, or you don't have the privacy you want), but rather to feed the baby with a bottle, then do that with the very same warmth and relaxation you would bring to breast feeding!

Mothers who have gone from breast feeding to the bottle, or who have breast fed but had someone else feed the baby a bottle when they were at work or away (or while they caught up on sleep) have noticed how little difference it makes to their baby *as long as the baby is being held the same way*. With bottle feeding, it's sometimes easier for the mother to be distracted by other people around, or by trying to do something else at the same time. You need to make a point of feeding your bottle baby just as if she were nursing. Keep the baby in very close to you, be alone, have the baby's skin against your skin, hold her firmly, give her your total attention for the first few months.

All feeding experiences, whether with breast or bottle, can be an emotional pleasure for both you and the new baby, a precious time for you to grow together. Through feeding, the baby can get food, plus sucking, plus contact comfort.

SUCKING

Every mother who has had a child on a pacifier (or a "plug" or a "dummy") knows that you never travel without an extra one! Pacifiers, like many childcare aids, are "in" or "out" depending on the year you have your baby. One experienced mother who has a 10- and a 13-year-old, just had a new baby. It's now 1 month old. She brought the baby to work. He sat happily in his plastic carrier sucking, dozing and sleeping while people worked all around him. The mother wasn't sure that pacifiers were approved by others, and when anyone stopped to comment on the darling baby, she quickly apologized: "I swore I'd never use a plug with my baby. I didn't for the others, but it keeps him so content that I use it when I'm working!" What she needs to know is that babies vary in their need for sucking. When they are being fed they are fulfilling their sucking needs as well as their hunger needs. For some babies, feeding is not enough to fulfill those sucking needs. The sucking drive varies from very strong to relatively mild. Some babies would suck anything in sight if only they could get it in their mouths. For others, it isn't a strong need, and they wouldn't suck a pacifier if you stuck it in their mouth. Sucking during the first year of life (including the thumb) is fulfilling a different need than after a year (time is approximate, of course). Sucking past the first year often fulfills the comforting need for holding and cuddling, as well as the sucking need. For those babies who, early in their life, can't fulfill their sucking needs through feeding, a pacifier is just right. But do be sure you have an extra one when the baby starts tossing it around or feeling brave without it. Some parents have driven all over a city in the middle of the night to buy a new pacifier! Without apology, notice the sucking needs of your baby and go with the baby rather than with how you think it may look to others. Sucking, just like eating, sleeping and being held close, is a natural need of your new baby.

SLEEPING

Before you have your baby, lots of mothers will tell you how easy the first three months are because your baby will sleep all of the time. Other mothers will tell you that your baby will be crying every night for the first few months. It may come as a surprise to you when your baby turns out differently and seems to be sleeping any time within every twenty-four hours. Just like grown-ups, babies vary in their need for sleep. Even so, up until 3 months, most babies *do* sleep most of the time (on their tummies).

It's exciting to notice the first few times your baby wakes up and plays in his crib before he cries out for food or for you. From 3 to 6 months he is awake more and more often. If he has a mobile or soft toy to look at, he will enjoy being by himself and looking around up to an hour or so. It's at this early age that babies learn to enjoy peace and quiet, just as they sometimes enjoy music, action and playing. A baby doesn't have to be constantly attended, have rock blasting through the house, or see a whirling mobile all of his waking hours. Starting at 6 months, try for a balance in the kinds of stimulation the baby has.

At around 6 months you can begin to adjust your baby's sleeping schedule. Some working parents like to keep their baby up late, so they can see them when they get home. Others like to put them to bed early so that the parents themselves can have some time alone. Some babies will go to bed early so that they will get up early; others late so that they will sleep late like the rest of the family. It's not always quite as easy as that, of course, because their feedings, sleeping and activities are changing so quickly. But still, the baby can adapt to the family from then on, in ways they couldn't before 6 months.

Should you always go to your baby when she wakes up at night? During the first year you always have to check out why your baby is crying. After 9 months (or a year), you will want to avoid spending much time with your child in the middle of the night. If you start getting water, or playing, or holding, or putting the baby in your room, you start rewarding your baby for waking up. Many babies wake up because of teething pains. Oftentimes they will go back to sleep if no one goes near them. Other times, they may need their gums rubbed or a soothing voice. Try and spend the minimum time with them at night. Between 1 and 2 years, you will want to help your baby with her need for a healthy separation from her parents. Being on their own at night is one step in that direction.

CRYING

Everybody wants to tell you why babies cry and what to do about it. You will hear that a baby cries to test her lungs. Or that he cried because he is hungry, or wet, or because he is a baby. You'll hear that you will spoil your baby if you go to her when she is crying: "It builds character to cry it out." Most mothers will admit that if they tried, they could *always* find a reason for why their baby cried. Often we just don't like the reason: they might be hungry before we think they should be, or they might want to get up sooner than we are ready to have them get up, or they might have gas pains after we've already heard one burp, or they might have taken on the anxiety of their mother because someone is coming to visit two minutes after they are supposed to be asleep. Or their mothers might be hoping to change their feeding and napping time pattern and stretch it out a little longer. Or their mother might otherwise have set up a crying situation. For example, the first time a 1-year-old falls and scrapes a knee or hits her head, or gets cold toes from lying in the snow too long, her mother might cry just looking at her, then the baby follows the example and cries too!

New babies cry because there is something to cry about. It is one of the few ways babies can get a parent's attention when parents are in another room, or doing something else in the same room. Crying is communication. Crying means something. It's up to the parent to find out what. You will enjoy these communications and start to be proud of yourself as you learn to figure out what the crying means—when you hear the burp, or they guzzle the milk or fruit juice, or they get up with all kinds of energy. You may decide to let them cry—knowing what you are doing—in order to encourage them to sleep through the night, or wait for the next meal. As long as you know that is what you are doing, and you time it so that you can stand it, you are still taking their cries seriously. Crying in the first few months is one place to learn observation skills, to learn to notice behavior. Crying is a place where you learn to be logical by going through all the possibilities that could have provoked the crying. Crying is your baby's talk to you. Communication with your baby starts at day one, with everything the baby does—and crying is one of the things the baby does best.

A SPACE FOR GROWING

Babies need an interesting place to be with things to look at, things to smell, things to listen to, things to touch. That doesn't mean they should be stimulated out of their minds with rattles shoved in their faces every minute, or with mobile cribs going at full swing all the time. But it does mean giving attention to their space. It's fun for parents to plan for the new baby's space, and it's good for the baby to have a stimulating environment.

A space for growing means a safe place. It means getting the obvious dangers at home out of the way: medicine, kitchen cleansers, razors and scissors. As your baby changes, your home has to change too. You

can childproof your home with gates at the top of the
stairs, gates at the doors, pot handles on the stove
turned away from a toddler, precious glass dishes re-
moved from the lower shelves.

Babies need to get out. As interesting as their room
is, or as safe as the rug is for crawling, an outdoor
stroller ride is good for both mama and baby—just for
the change. The change in air, in smells, in things to
look at, and a place for the unexpected to happen. You
won't need special places to go with the baby. You
won't need to spend money to be entertained by some
event. It's just out to see the wonders of the world—
trees, adults of all sizes and shapes, birds, children of
all ages and behavior, flowers, different kinds of dogs
and all sizes of buildings.

One of the natural needs of children is an accepting
familyplace to try out their ideas, to be creative, to
learn to live with others in the family. A space for
growing. Creating this space within the family is as
much a parent's responsibility as putting food on the
table. Watching your baby respond to a growing and
learning environment will be as fulfilling to you as
watching her gain weight and grow strong.

TLC

During the first year of life, the baby needs to be
held very close very often. He needs TLC (tender loving care). The more he gets the better. Holding and affection needs during the first year of life are almost as
strong as the need for food. There is no such thing as
too much affection. Just think of your own affection
needs and you will quickly recognize that you aren't
spoiled with too much of it.

During the baby's bath time he receives tactile im-
pressions—he learns to feel good about his body. He
has fun and he feels good. He learns to think that, if he
feels good, he *must* be "good." *Express your affection
at this age.* Many psychiatrists have learned that you
can't make up at age 10 for the lack of physical affection at age 1. Holding and comforting your baby is a

specific need. It should be given as much thought and attention from the beginning as you give the baby's food and sleep needs.

PATIENCE AND TRUST

You can't spoil a baby during the first six months. Crying babies at this age are *not* manipulating you to get what they want. The baby is just expressing her need—sometimes louder than you wish, but she has not yet learned to think out what she is trying to get you to do. A baby under 6 months is *not* in a power-play situation with you. Babies learn about frustrations and not getting what they need: food, being held up for a burp, getting warmer or cooler air, being held a lot at this early age. Research has shown that the more a baby's needs are met in his first 6 months, the better he can cope with frustrations and learn to be patient when he wants something at a later age. So don't keep what you know your baby wants from her because you are afraid of spoiling her—especially in her first 6 months. The way to teach trust in people, and to teach patience and the ability to cope with frustrations in an imperfect world, is to meet the physical and emotional needs of your baby as well as you can see them. There will always be needs unmet—those needs you *don't* perceive—just as there are unmet needs in all of your relationships. You are teaching your baby to trust that his needs will be met. When your baby does learn to trust, he can relax and afford to wait a while for his food, his hug, or getting up in the morning. Daily care with TLC is what the first 6 months of a baby are all about. TLC builds. It's contagious. Giving it turns out to be developmental for you, too.

SHAPE UP
OR WATCH OUT!

You *are* going to clean your room . . . or you are *not* going out tonight! You *are* going to study right now, or you are *not* going to the basketball game. You *are* going to take care of your little brother, or you are *not* getting any allowance this week. You *are* coming home right this minute, or you are *never* going to use the car again! You are *not* going to smoke in this house! Smack! Swat! Whack!

Discipline. Every teenager knows what that means. You've got to shape up or watch out. All your privileges can suddenly go flying out the window. When everyone in the family is down on you, life can be really miserable.

As you think about how your parents try to shape you up, about what you like and what you hate about it, as you look at what works with you and what is impossible for you to live with, you can begin to think through what kind of parent *you* want to be. What kind of rules will *you* make for your kids, your teenagers? What works best with you? What do you resent most? When did you first notice what kind of discipline your parents used on you? What kinds of power do you have that works for you? When did all of these rules for shaping up begin?

DISCIPLINE STARTS AT BIRTH

The best discipline is preventive. Discipline that
works starts because of a climate of cooperation in
your family. As you read about TLC in this book, you
see how your baby learns that she can depend on you
for her first needs of eating, sleeping, being held and
being comforted. Your baby will listen best to you
when she is a little older because you listened to her as
an infant. Trust grows and builds. Cooperation is the
outcome of trust.

As much as children and teenagers sometimes hate
the rules, they hate being without them even worse.
Discipline means establishing rules and setting limits
for each member living together in the family. Being
without rules and boundaries implies that no one cares
enough to make the rules, that no one cares enough to
carry them out and, even worse, that no one thinks you
are worthy of rules to begin with.

RULES AND LIMITS ARE GUIDELINES

Rules, like maps and guides, help you to know
where you are going. They make you feel sure. Secure.
In order to feel good about guidelines and rules, you
will want and need to be in on them. And you should
be. As a daughter, you may well feel that you are on
the powerless end of rule establishment. Even so, you
are probably aware of the skills you have developed to
get what you want in dealing with power struggles with
your parents. When you become the mother, you have
to turn all of that power around. When you become the
mother, *you* will be on the power end of the discipline.

DISCIPLINE IS BUILT ON RESPECT

Discipline starts at birth when the baby learns to
trust and depend on you, but it continues to grow only
if you show your baby and little toddler that you respect him. It's just like any other relationship—respect

is the center for cooperation and a growing friendship. Just because a person is tiny and very young doesn't mean that you can live happily together without respect. A lot of mothers have never thought of the respect idea when it comes to their own children. Just watch some mothers with young children grab their child's arm and sweep them off their feet to hurry them along, never saying please or thank you to their kids but expecting their children to say it, or slapping the hand of a 2-year-old because she spilled some Coke in the pizza parlor from a glass too large for her in the first place.

Some ways to show respect to a 2-year-old, for example, include not scolding, yelling or punishing the child in front of others, not interrupting when he is talking, knocking on his door before you go in, and asking if you can look at his paintings before you snatch them out of his hand to show to someone else. Respect has to be part of your discipline if you expect it to "take" and be a part of his. As a teenager you can well understand this idea, because you know how much you need the respect of *your* parents when they come down hard on you. When you become a mother, you will have to give the same kind of respect to your children that you need from others.

DISCIPLINE HAS TO MAKE SENSE

No matter how much cooperation and respect you have started with, young children will still need to be corrected—and corrected with the appropriate punishment. Discipline has to make sense for the age of the child and the misbehavior involved. Up until 6 months, you try to give enough milk, a good place to sleep, and to answer the cries by finding out what the problem is *as best you can. There is no such thing as correcting an infant.* The infant is not aware of what you want it to do. Punishment before 6 months does not make sense. When the baby starts to move around, life is another matter. You can't be shouting *no* all day long, and yet it won't make sense to keep a baby confined all the time, squelching her curiosity. That doesn't make sense either. After all, you *do* want to raise an independent and curious person. But making a childproof room or space where the baby can move around does make sense. It gives both you and the baby more freedom— freedom for the baby to explore, and freedom for you to relax without allowing the baby to break up the household.

When the baby is around one year and does get into everything, "substitution" is the key word and action. Instead of grabbing the screwdriver you left on the table out of her hand, get the rattle and swap it. When she seizes your china coffee cup and wings it in mid-air, hand the baby her own plastic cup. You can get away with substituting anything and everything at this age.

By the time your baby is about 18 months old, you will see that you can make a rule and expect your baby to follow it . . . *most of the time.* Let's say the rule is that your baby cannot be on the stairs without you. With a very young child you must be sure you have communicated the rule. You can't be vague about it. Get close to your child, take her hand or touch her arm or shoulder, look her straight in the eye and when you have her undivided attention, say very clearly, "No, you cannot go upstairs." Repeat it during the week, and expect it to take a few days to sink in. Later, you will probably hear your toddler going busily around the house repeating the rules exactly as you have said them. Often at nap- or nighttime, a young child practises saying the rules over and over just before going to sleep, as they practice the new words they heard during the day.

When the baby does try the stairs, even though she is clear about the rule, and you see her when she is halfway up, don't yank her down, spank or holler at her and scare her to death. An extreme punishment doesn't make sense to a child, it only horrifies a tiny baby and makes her anxious. When they are anxious, young children act out (misbehave), which is what you are trying to avoid. You are not trying to frighten your baby, but you must take *some* appropriate action for breaking the rule. After all, if a rule is broken and there is no consequence, future rules—and threats about the rules—will have no meaning. Punishment must make sense to your child. For example, until three, some punishments that do make sense are sitting in a chair for fifteen minutes, no favorite toy for an hour, no ice cream, standing in a corner for five minutes. You will be surprised how long fifteen minutes is to a 2-year-old, and you will also learn that five to fifteen minutes is all that is needed for getting your point across, and showing your disapproval.

SHAPING UP THE BABY

How do you go about figuring out how you will shape up your baby? Chances are, you will discipline your baby exactly as you were disciplined—even if you think the way your parents disciplined you was unfair and didn't work. Before you can make any real changes in the way you want to shape up your own kids, you have to make a real effort to find out what it is you don't like about your parents' discipline—what doesn't feel right to you, what isn't fair, what makes you angry rather than cooperative. What's wrong with it? Why doesn't it work?

If you can figure out what your parents want, and what they are trying to get from you, it will be easier for you to figure out what you will do with your own kids. Parents threaten to take away everything you need—freedom to go out, use of the car, money. But some parents never pull it off. Other parents carry through every threat for every rule their children break. Most parents are somewhere in between about enforcing the law, and it's sometimes probably hard for you to know if you've got a good chance to call their bluff and get away with it—or if you haven't. Of course experience helps. By this time you've put in a lot of years at home with your parents, and you're probably pretty good at observing them. You can probably predict quite well what you can get away with and what rules you have to follow to the letter.

TEENAGE POWER

No matter what type of parents you have, chances are that none of them are going to let you do everything you want to do all of the time. Chances are, too, that you are financially dependent on them. You count on your family for food, a home, a car, clothes and money. With all the responsibility they take for you, parents usually want control over what you do. In other words, they seem to have *all* the power. But you've got some things *they* want too. Like affection, approval, cooperation at home with all the things that need to be done in a family, such as mowing the lawn, cooking, running errands, shoveling snow, shopping, taking care of brothers and sisters, writing to relatives, buying family gifts and so on. Also, parents usually want you to do well in school. A lot of your power is in being the kind of teenage daughter they think you should be. And some of these things you will want for yourself, too. Like decent grades, good friends, experience and skills in school activities such as music, sports, dramatics and publications. You have a student kind of power. You can negotiate getting some of the things you want by being clear about the kinds of student and social skills you are learning, skills that contribute to your family's pride and image.

TAKE THE TEST

Take the "Shaping You Up" test. If you are in class, get a discussion going with your classmates, or with others in a group or club. Or take the test alone, and get a friend to take it, too. If you really want to see sparks fly, let your parents take the test, and discuss it with them! The more you share your ideas, the clearer you will become about "what's going on around here" when it comes to shaping you up.

SHAPING YOU UP

Who tries to shape you up?
Mother

Father
Brother
Sister
Grandparent
Aunt
Uncle
No one
Combination of above
Other_____

Why do they try to shape you up?
To make you better
For your safety
To make you more independent
To make you more dependent
To control you
To get rid of their anger
To make the family look good
For your health
So you won't make the mistakes they made
For prestige
They're worried about what others think
To improve family relationships
You're not up to their standards
You bug them
To prevent crime
Other_____

What do they do to shape you up?
Nag
Yell
Cry
Lecture
Punch you
Hit you
Shove you
Push you
Give you the silent treatment
Fume
Humiliate you
Take away: car
　　TV
　　night out
　　allowance

    phone
    sports
    being with friends
    other_____
Ignore you
Give you an earlier bedtime
Threaten you
Give you extra work at home
Tease you
Send you: to your room
    outdoors
    to a closet
    to the cellar
    to sit in a special place
Call a family meeting

Where do you act out?
  Home
  School
  Church
  Community
  Car
  Other_____

When do they shape you up?
  After: bad grades
    smoking
    drinking
    drugs
    staying out too late
    bad posture
    eating junk food
    sex-related activities
    fighting with brother or sister
    failing to put things away
    slamming doors
    swearing
    wearing sloppy clothes
    keeping a sloppy room
    messing up the house
    not doing family chores
    not eating certain foods at the table
    bad manners

> bad report from school
> not going to church
> driving too fast
> too much TV
> being lazy
> leaving the milk out
> locking the bathroom door
> locking your bedroom door
> entering a room without knocking
> raiding the refrigerator
> teasing a sister or brother
> talking back
> disobeying family rules
> not listening
> blasting rock music through the house
> breaking something
> spilling something
> not writing a thank-you letter
> Other_____

How do you react to their discipline?

Hitting a punching bag
Screaming
Locking yourself in your room
Reading
Sulking
Yelling back
Cooperating
Hitting back
Slamming doors
Kicking the dog
Swearing
Working it off
Ignoring it
Telling a friend
Denying it
Getting even
Hitting a sister or brother
Taking it out on a sister or brother
Jogging
Shaping up!
Other_____

WHO NEEDS IT?

If discipline means that you must constantly be figuring out how to shape up the baby to live in a family with others who have needs and rights, too; if discipline means that your baby has to have rules so that others in the family will enjoy his style of interaction and feel his respect for everyone else, then, *everyone* in a family needs discipline. When the *child* doesn't shape up, you must constantly be figuring out the "Watch Out!" part below—the consequences of the punishment for the youngster and for the rest of the family.

WATCH OUT!

One of the messages your children will learn from you is *how* you shape them up. Children learn more than the message that they are not to climb the stairs, or cross the street or clean the toilet with your toothbrush. They also learn your reaction to misbehavior and how you deal with the frustration of children who are not behaving exactly as you wish. They learn about anger, *your* anger. And theirs in reaction to yours. They learn about conflict, about wanting to please you and also wanting to do it their way. They learn about your conflicts—saying you love them one minute, and yelling at them the next. About your wanting peace and quiet and choosing to have 3 children under 5 in your family, if that's what you chose to do.

ANGER

Children bring out our most loving selves. We often can be much more loving to our babies and children, then we can be to our parents, or even to our husbands. The combination of that tiny baby being so dependent upon us, needing us so much, being our very own kind, the romanticism about having a baby in our lives, and our genuine wish to be open and warm and close with another person, all lead to expressing our love.

We don't hear as often that our children bring out our most hateful selves, our most angry and violent and rageful selves. And because we don't hear so much about them, it isn't easy to handle these negative emotions. It may help if you know that just about all parents have these feelings. Most parents who spend much time with their children would like to strike out at them at one time or another. Having feelings of anger and rage is not the problem. But what we do about these feelings, how we act on them, is. Usually, expressing anger and hate and rage directly isn't even acceptable toward someone our own age—much less toward some little kid or baby! One mother expressed her fear about how she felt this way:

> "Wow! I really need to know how other people feel about their children. When my two boys get in a fight, I just can't stand them . . . I think they are little monsters or animals, and I wonder where they came from. How did they get into *my* family? I wonder if other mothers feel like this. Do they worry about not loving their kids all the time? Or *do* they always love their kids? I never heard anyone else say, 'I just can't stand my kids.' How can I feel good about myself, and about my kids, when I just can't stand them when they fight?"

Another mother of a 2- and a 3-year-old said:

> "I'll never forget it! Over ten years ago I was in a bookstore trying to concentrate on finding a book for a special friend as my kids raced between the book shelves. Everyone else was as quiet as if they were in a library. When I got outside, I smacked my son on the side of the head. The blow and surprise dropped him to his knees on the sidewalk. My anger had taken over. Anger that I had to have two loud kids running around a bookstore when I really needed to be alone. But what I remember most is not being able to handle

my anger. It's still on my mind. What kind of a mother smacks her kid, when the kid is only acting like an active three-year-old?"

What can parents do? We can recognize that having and expressing negative feelings is a part of family life. Family life is full of angry situations. If you saw *Saturday Night Fever,* you saw a wonderful example of family hitting, throwing things and shouting at each other. At the dinner table the father hit John Travolta on the back of the head for every disagreement he had with him, while his mother took food away from his father and he threw his meat at his mother.

It's especially hard to handle anger because we know that spouses "should" love each other, parent's "should" feel nothing but love for their children, and children "should" respect their parents.

Conflict comes when we know how we are expected to act, but we give in instead to our negative feelings and we act quite the opposite. One thing that helps is to acknowledge that all people have negative feelings. Negative feelings are as old as Bible stories. Everybody has them. Another thing that helps is not to hide your emotions. If you get angry, you don't have to scream, but you can still let people know that you're angry. "Mommy is very angry, even though she's trying not to take it out on you." If it's out in the open, children can get out of the way, for one thing. And they can also learn that when *they* get angry, they can talk about it.

Learning to live with conflict is something we all have to do. "Resolving" conflicts only happens in the psychiatrist's office. The rest of us have learned that conflicts are here to stay. Talking about conflict as clearly as we learn to see it, asking each family member to try to support our positive actions and to forgive our negative behavior as we try to change it, is the best we can do.

BASIC TRAINING

Little children learn to handle their conflicts, to be cooperative and respectful, or violent, in their own families, from their own parents. Just as children who are shown respect learn to be respectful, children who are abused learn to become abusive parents and adults. Their own family has provided them with the basic training for violence or for cooperation. Research by sociologist Richard J. Gelles, who wrote *The Violent Home,* shows that children learn the details of how to act at home, even when it's a negative action like violence. The family is the social institution for teaching values and how to act. Children learn how to love and they learn also how to hit, what to hit with, where to hit, how much it should hurt, and when it's OK to be violent. They learn that when someone "deserves" to be hit, it's called "normal violence." Linda, 15, told about so-called normal violence when she described protecting her younger friend:

> "I hate it when every man thinks he's got the right to beat up on his wife and kids. I've got this friend I like a lot. She is twelve years old. She calls me Big Sis 'cause if anybody ever hurt her, I'd kill 'im—and I almost did. Her father hit her, so I whammmmmmm—right on the head with an iron frying pan. It shocked him (laughs). It shocked me, too."

Children grow up to be respectful of others, or to be violent, when they watch cooperation, or violence, between their parents, or feel it used on them, or see it between their brothers and sisters. When they grow up with violence they don't like it, but they learn that to physically strike out is a solution—even though they say they hate violence. Sharon, 14, demonstrates the lesson very well:

> "When I was a little kid my mother hit me a lot, you know, when I didn't do something I was supposed to do, or when I talked back, or when I

didn't eat my dinner, or when I was in trouble with her. But ever since I turned twelve, my mother has never hit me. Well, she hit me once, but I put her through the picture window."

And Debbie, a 15-year-old, said she wasn't getting married because:

"Well, my mother went through two husbands and got beat up by both of them all the time. The woman next door is always getting beat up by her husband, and she is always running to my house and I see what it looks like. So the first time that a guy hits *me*—I'm going to send him through a wall. Case closed!"

WHAT IS VIOLENCE?

Violence is a copout. It's the opposite of coping. Violence is a negative solution or response to frustration and stress. It's acting out, or striking out, to whoever is smaller than you—including the people who are closest to you. Even pets. Violence is slapping, threatening, pushing, punching, kicking, and throwing objects at someone. It's abusing people. Violence is also indecent sexual activity such as incest.

Probably the most common form of violence isn't hitting at all, but excessive yelling, shouting and teasing. Many homes are "noise-violent" all of the time. The parents shout at each other and at the kids, and the kids shout at each other and back at the parents.

Striking a child is not considered violent by many parents. Usually it's thought of as an outbreak of uncontrolled anger. Many parents consider a spanking or a slap on the child's hand a good way to teach a lesson—within the rules of the family.

Violence is the result of not coping with the frustrations of family life. It's misbehaving instead. It's a copout from sitting down and working things out in the family. It's a copout from working for each person's rights in the family. Your rights!

HOW DOES VIOLENCE HAPPEN?

One common condition that increases the chances for violence is that the parents are immature and they really don't understand their child's needs. They often expect babies to act like adults. To eat and sleep more like their parents do. When parents don't relate well to other adults, they often hope that their own baby will make up for the adult company they are not getting. Of course a baby can't ever make up for what the parent hasn't worked out for herself or himself. Many abusive parents don't have a clue about child development, and really have no idea about how to raise a child. Or how to handle a child. They don't know what to do for a crying baby, and they don't know that a baby needs to be held often and close.

At this point in your life—if you want to do all you can to prevent violence in your home—learn about child development and how to care for babies. Learn how to be a friend and express yourself to your friends. Work on your own self-esteem and your understanding of others. The key to creating a safe and thriving environment is seeing respect and human rights as basic needs for you and for every member of your family. Human rights, respect and cooperation are the guarantee against violence . . . a guarantee for a loving family.

SHAPED UP FEELS GOOD

When you, as a teenager, can live by the rules in your family, you know how good it feels. And when you can't, you know how awful it can be. You know when you are out of synch with your parents. Try to use this same understanding with your own baby, as early as you can. As a young mother, try to remember how important it was to you, as a daughter, to be in on the rules—to have discipline make sense. Remember how it really did feel good when everyone in the family was shaping up!

HUMAN RIGHTS ARE THE RIGHTS OF CHILDREN

by Virginia Coigney

The public as a whole is not interested, in fact they are repelled, by the idea that children have rights separate from those of their parents. The truth is that the most influential force in the attainment of civil rights for young people is apt to be you, the mother.

If you are the mother of a small child, or simply thinking about becoming a mother, you are also very likely taking on the role of property owner. The property in this instance is your child. Before you reject this definition of the mother-child relationship, let's investigate our real feelings about children and, in particular, let's look at our feelings about our very own children. Here are some questions to help you to think about your attitudes about children:

1. Do you laugh or smile when you see a child cry?
2. Do you talk about children and their friends in their presence?
3. Do you reserve for yourself the right to make major life decisions for your child?
4. Do you believe that it is your child's duty to love you? To obey you?
5. Do you think your child's obedience and love is the proper trade-off for your love and protection?

6. Do you listen to what children are trying to tell you?

7. Do you respect a child's feelings of jealousy, fear, disappointment?

8. Do you believe they should participate in decisions affecting them insofar as they are able?

9. Do you believe they have a right to a fair portion of the family resources?

10. Do you respect equally children of all races, colors and creeds, or do you suspect that children who are very different from your own are less "valuable"?

If you answered "no" to questions 1 through 5, and "yes" to questions 6 through 10, you have or will have a most fortunate child. Simple as children may seem, they make it impossible to conceal a bias for or against the given child as a separate human bring. And it is this concept of separateness that we must accept before we can accept children as free beings whose care and safety we are responsible for—for only a specific period of time. Parenting can be a rewarding responsibility, but it keeps changing because its purpose is to work toward independence. Insofar as we assist the child to grow up—and, to a large degree, away from us, we are successful in our parenting.

This is not an easy thing to do. The child we carry remains a part of our bodies long after the cord is cut. To some degree it is the same for the child. The discovery that mother's hand is not simply an extension of the child's own hand is one of the early steps in the child's development. Still, the mother's sense of the child as part of herself persists. She is glad, ashamed, proud, vindicated, made whole by the existence and, of course, the behavior of the child. In this she acutely feels the child as "hers."

Children's Feelings

In order to encourage the separateness that is critical to growing children, we have to learn to respect children as real people. Very few adults respect the feelings of children. Adults laugh at youthful attempts at love and friendship; repress young efforts at touching and meeting. A child's tears are common cause of amusement or anger.

We criticize the way the child looks and behaves. We call attention to faults and failures in a brutal stream of comment. We feel free to question a child's honesty, dreams, her thoughts, and her friendships. Furthermore, we ask her to believe that we say these things for her own good. Since children believe a good deal of what we tell them, we have to notice what we say.

Yet it isn't difficult to run up a list of things that lead both adults and children to rage and sometimes tears. Jealousy, lovelessness, fear, feelings of inadequacy, unjust criticism, plans gone awry, threats, violence, loss of a valued object. What makes such circumstances matters of great seriousness when they occur among adults, and unimportant when experienced by children, is difficult to see, and yet the answer is painfully obvious. The distinguishing factor is power. Children's feelings are less important because they have little power. Like prisoners or suppressed minorities or dependent women, they get their power by association and often by the difficulties they can create. The child's status, like that of the dependent wife, is generally determined by those "others"—husbands or parents—who have power.

To deny the validity of children's feelings is to reject their humanity. If we are to admit children to the kingdom of "real people," if we are to respect them, value their individuality and their uniqueness, we must, of course, plan to set them free.

Discipline, rather than child development, is of most interest to parents. The child who will not "mind" is an indescribable threat to the parent, a source of irritation and often blind rage. Perfectly intelligent, well-balanced men and women turn to screaming hysterics in the face of a child's misbehavior. A visit to any park or playground will quickly demonstrate adults' dislike for children and a reason for it. Children are stubborn. Children are uncontrollable. Children are unreasonable. Child are irritating and difficult, all of which is a way

of saying that children very often do not readily do
what adults wish them to do.

What actually is at stake for the adult whose authority is flaunted by a child? Why is her anger so dispro-
portionate? Parents say they get angry because they
feel powerless when a child acts out: they can't walk
away from the responsibility; they are jealous of the
child's freedom.

The child's refusal to accept authority is a sharp re-
minder of the parent's daily helplessness—in work, in
marriage, in so many relationships.

In order to respect the feelings of children we have
to learn how they feel. Anyone can know how children
feel. They feel pretty much as we do. Perhaps that's
the probelm. Perhaps we cannot respect the feelings of
children because we have never learned to respect our
own feelings, especially our feelings about children.

A New Mother
and Children's Rights

Learning to accept a child's separate existence isn't
automatic. It's about the last thing a new mother has on
her mind. I well remember my own shock when I
found that the baby I had produced bore little resem-
blance to the Gerber-baby-food ad which until that
moment had been my model for infancy. Raised by a
grandmother, working at 15 and a mother at 19, I had
only the vaguest notion of what a baby looked like before I had one—and no idea at all of how babies acted.
My daughter Mary's independent will, right from birth,
was a complete and not altogether pleasant surprise. I
had thought, if indeed I *had* thought about the matter
at all, that my baby would be warm and cuddly,
sweet-smelling and perpetually smiling. Moreover, I
had taken it for granted that the baby would adore
me—always.

The actuality was somewhat different. Mary was a
problem feeder from the beginning. I did not have the
support which, as I look back, I greatly needed if I
were to successfully nurse. Mary could not digest her

formula and was hungry and wailing a good deal of the time during those first few weeks. Successive feedings rested for a while in her outraged little stomach only to erupt in whale-like demonstrations which left her anxious mother and the tiny apartment's furnishings equally drenched. If she adored me she gave little sign of it. Cuddly she was not.

That she lived to grow up into a marvelous human being with whom I have an enviable relationship happened despite miserable beginnings. Handicapped as I was by equal parts of impatience and ignorance, it is probably luck that she lived to grow up. If anyone had come around selling children's rights to me during my first brush with motherhood, I should have thrown up my hands and screamed, and seen no connection between rights and motherhood at all.

Not even seven years and another daughter later, could I have considered the idea of children's rights with anything except intellectual interest for other mothers. By this time I had practiced, but by no means perfected, the art of mothering, and my second child, Ann, was spared many but not all of my earlier bumblings.

But children's rights! I thought of my children as *my* children. I gave them privileges, but withheld rights. In this I followed the practice of rulers everywhere. Liberty was used as a reward—or a bribe. It did not cross my mind that the children had rights which I might prevent them from exercising, but which they had whether I recognized them or not—with their status as human beings.

Change the World

As human beings, children have the right to nourishing food, adequate shelter and clothing, special protection, health care and education. Love and understanding are also assumed to be rights of the child.

The sad truth is that the world's children are, for the most part ill-housed, ill-clothed and ill-fed. They suffer from debilitating illnesses which often handicap them for life. They bear more than their share of the ravages of poverty, crime and war. We do not have to travel out of our own country to realize the truth of these statements.

But you are not thinking of changing the world. You are thinking of having a baby. Surely one can still have a baby without taking on the problems of all human-kind! Perhaps, but not easily. To have a child is to take out an option on the future. What happens to the world's children becomes more important when you have children of your own. This is partly because then you sometimes "feel" closer to children, and the problems of children become more real to you. But it is also true because you gradually sense that part of your responsibility as a parent lies in the preparation of the world your child will live in, grow up in, raise children in.

And so we come full circle to the question of children's rights. What are they? Who is to assure them? Insofar as children are wholly dependent on the generosity of adults for their rights and their needs, they will go without both a great deal of the time. You may feel quite capable of meeting the physical needs of your own children. You may subscribe in part or in whole to children's rights. You may be so emotionally mature and loving and giving that child development centers are named after you. You may be. But chances are that you are like most new mothers—excited, scared, uncertain. If that is the case perhaps you'll want to do a good deal of soul searching before you take on the joyous, frightening, wonderful, aggravating, happy, painful responsibility of a human life—other than your own.

THE RIGHTS OF CHILDREN

Before you decide to have a baby, you will want to spend some time learning a little about how children grow. You should have some idea of what to expect and when to expect it. You will want to review the needs of children and determine whether or not you can within reason meet those needs.

And you will want to think long and carefully about children's rights. Does the phrase make you think at once of ill-mannered, demanding spoiled brats? If it does you have a way to go. Discipline and consideration for others is far more apt to occur under conditions of liberty than under those of repression. If respect for the feelings and needs of others is taught by example rather than by force, one may expect that behavior to become a part of the child's developing personality.

The rights of children, however, extend beyond the courtesies, and it takes patience, strength and dedication to parenting to honor children's rights by more than words alone. The first requirement is to accept the idea that children, because they are human creatures, do have certain rights which it is *within your power to insure*. First and foremost they have a right to your parenting. By caring for them and sharing your life and your resources with them, you are not doing them a favor. You are fulfilling your own freely selected decision to be a parent. If you go about this sharing of your life and resources fairly and wisely, you will have little trouble with the concepts of children's rights. The child who is treated as a full member of the family is, however, seldom a reality. This is not intended to imply that the child's wishes should take precedence over everyone else's in matters of family life. But they should be considered. The child's desires are not ridiculous simply because they are childlike.

A child's "rights" does not mean simply getting her own way. (But then, even this is no worse then the parent who always insists on the last word.) Your child's safety must always take precedence in any family decision—whether or not the child sees it that way. But you must learn to examine your motivations carefully. Are you sure that you are insisting on a certain course of action for the child's sake or for your own sake?

Most importantly, can you acknowledge the right of a child to the validity of his feelings? Can you accept the child's need for privacy? Can you accept the child who is different? Do you respect real children as well as those you read about or see from a distance? All of these and many other factors go into the concept of the rights of children. But if we are looking for a definition, we might try this one: "When we speak of a child's rights, we refer to human rights which exist by virtue of membership in the human race." These rights are no less important because of the child's age and greater need.

In all considerations about the rights of children it is urgent that we extend our concern beyond our own children. Must we try to change the world just because we are planning to have a baby? The answer to that question has to be an unqualified "yes." We must do what we can to make the world a decent place for children to be born, to live in, to work and love in.

Here, too, we must be mindful of the rights of children. Who more than they have the right to take part in the work of making the world a better place? By engaging their interest and enthusiasm in this effort, we will especially honor their humanity and help to give them that greatest human right—a worthwhile idea to live by.

A FAMILY-PLACE

When you are in school, sometimes it seems like the workplace is more important than the familyplace. You hear more about how to plan to get a job, what kind of work possibilities there are, how much money everyone makes at work, and how important a meaningful career is in your life than you do about where you live.

Unless you are in a family-living course, you hear very little in school about the importance of the familyplace. The place where you will raise your children. The place where all adults come from. The place where little children learn what it's OK to feel like, what it's OK to act like, what is an OK way to treat others, and what is an OK way to be treated by others. Teaching these crucial life-learning experiences to our children is probably the most important job in the world, as psychiatrist Dr. Helen DeRosis shows in "Growing Children Need Growing Parents" below.

Career and life planning have to include your parenting career. Parenting takes place in the family. As you think about becoming a mother, don't try to choose between the workplace and the familyplace. If you are a mother, you *will* have a familyplace. In addition, you will also have a workplace. Prepare yourself for your total career. For women, that means designing the kind of place you most want to be a part of—your familyplace.

GROWING CHILDREN NEED GROWING PARENTS*

by Helen DeRosis, M.D.

It is probably safe to say that more people are parents than anything else. And while parenting is one of the most important jobs in the world, it is one for which very little training has been provided. I suppose it's been assumed that since so many people are likely to become parents, they would manage somehow to bumble their way through parenthood. Unfortunately, this is what has happened in too many instances. People have bumbled through as their parents did, and as their parents' parents did.

A strong argument in favor of the bumbling method has been the use of the good old maternal, or parental, instinct. I believe with others, however, that this instinct is not as reliable as it has been made out to be through the years. And certainly the many instances of child abuse bear that out repeatedly.

If a mother's instinct told her how to rear her young, then she would also instinctively know how to let the child grow in such a way as to permit it to develop its essential independence from her *at a proper pace*. In this way, she would not produce one of the many troubled children we find today.

*"Growing Children Need Growing Parents" was excerpted and adapted from Dr. DeRosis' book *Parent Power: Child Power*.

Parenthood Is Not
a Natural State

The basic nurturing that instinct might provide for one's young is simply not adequate to deal with living in our society today. But what about the parents who do an adequate job? Where do they learn? They did not have to go to school to become educated in how to be a good mother or father. Nor does one necessarily have to go to school to be a good historian or mathematician. If a child has someone in the home who is adept in these subjects, then she may learn there. But if no one at home knows anything about them, nothing can be learned unless one goes out to learn. And so those fortunate people who have had kind, self-respecting parents have learned from them.

Respect is a basic ingredient in family living. Where does love come in? The fact is that one cannot love when one does not respect. Parent-child feelings can become very complex and confused. What passes for love is often a lot of other feelings within the range of human responses. But I believe that love can grow upon respect in almost any relationship, if given half a chance.

These are some of the reasons why I say that parenthood is not a natural state. Although they become biological parents at the moment of their child's birth, people do not suddenly become parents in any comprehensive sense. People are not educated as parents. There are few effective programs that prepare one for parenthood. For the most part, motherhood is suddenly thrust upon you and you may naively believe that you are prepared for it by virtue of having experienced pregnancy and delivery.

Well-meaning, smiling relatives say nothing about the trials and tribulations of parenthood. They have either forgotten or they don't want to worry you. In either case, they are to be forgiven, but not depended upon. Relatives either give too much advice or too little. If they give too much, you hate to ask them anything. If too little, you hate to ask, because you think you should know it all.

Childhood
Is A Natural State

Contrary to the unnatural state of parenthood, childhood is a natural state. Children do not have to learn how to be children. They just are, without trying. It's all they have to be, while motherhood is imposed on top of everything else you are by the time you achieve that status.

Because a child automatically needs a parent (and let's not forget that!) he is perhaps the person who can best guide you about being a mother. He doesn't say, "Look, Mom, this is the way to do it," but the messages are there if you will look for them. The process of teaching and learning is a reversible one, however, with the child or the parent in the role of teacher, depending upon who starts what. The child either learns or teaches as the need arises, because he is doing just what comes naturally. But you are not as flexible. You have to learn every step of the way. This requires a deliberate approach that is very different from the natural approach of the child.

However, once you have learned how to be a mother to an infant—lo and behold she is no longer an infant. She is a playful, wakeful baby who wants much more of your time. And once you learn how to be a parent to a 9-month-old baby—presto chango!—she is a toddler.

At that point, very little of your previous expertise is of much use, for the toddler is a completely different person. A world of crib, carriage, playpen, bathinette, and other such limited areas suddenly changes into the entire house, the sidewalk, street and unlimited horizons. Once a child is mobile under her own power, it's another ball game.

When Baby is running about, things become more hectic. Baby wants more only because his horizons have expanded so. The parent does not know just how far Baby can go. When there is a difference between what Baby thinks he can do and what Mother thinks Baby can do, trouble starts. Baby tries to convey information to Mother, but she cannot understand it. Either she is not listening, not looking or just not patient enough. It doesn't take more than average intelligence to be a fairly successful parent. But it takes a tremendous amount of listening and adjusting.

In essence, then, you become a new parent with every new phase your child goes through—the wonderful phases, the terrible and the terrific times, the friendly and fearful ones. Each year brings you a new kind of child. But who can be a new parent each year? Who *wants* to be a new parent each year? Maybe you *will* want to if you know it is necessary, and if you are watching for the signals you are given as your child changes.

Supermom Is Impossible

Over fifteen years ago I began to work with groups of parents in schools and community centers. These parents were concerned about the quality of their parenting, and they wanted to do as much as they could to help their children learn and grow. As I worked with them, many expressed feelings of inadequacy about their functioning as parents. Not only that, but they usually felt guilty because of their limitations.

Their guilt was often two-sided. Where children had even a small problem, parents felt that they had done something to cause the problem; furthermore, they felt neglectful in not having prevented it. So they were blaming themselves for doing too much—in causing the difficulty—and too little in not preventing it. Such feelings lead to self-blaming, which contributes to a form of circular thinking, escape from which parents often find extremely difficult, if not impossible. To try to get rid of these feelings, parents often seek help from experts. In doing so, however, they try to use the experts' suggestions as *the* way for them, without selecting those suggestions which are compatible with their own background, personalities and family needs. To be useful, a suggestion must be filtered through your own evaluating system. It is for you to accept or reject. Only then can it have meaning and value within the context of your own family.

As the parent, you are in the best position to be the *primary person* for preventing your child's discontent and learning or behavior disorders. No one else is so available, so intimate, so committed, so powerful as you. This is true not only during the early years, but throughout adolescence and young adulthood. If you can appreciate this, you will be more interested in the quality of your parenting.

Satisfactory parenthood has to be worked at. Having a child and seeing it through babyhood is only one small step, usually the easiest. It's like planting flowers. Once they are in the ground, they need attention, or the blossoms will be skimpy. Sun and water aren't enough. For children, food, shelter, clothing and other objects aren't enough. They need mothers and fathers who are working at their parenting. *Growing children need growing parents.* It is difficult to imagine the satisfactory growth of a child without the parallel growth of a parent. Ideally, they develop and grow together.

What helps is a real understanding of your power and of your child's power. If you can rid yourself of traditional worries, guilt-ridden self-views, and anxiety-laden attitudes toward children's venturing, then you approach the possibility of pleasure in watching the unfolding of your child's unique possibilities.

In parents' discussion groups, we discussed and explored our own roles as parents—at times severely limited, ineffectual, inexperienced, inarticulate, afraid, at times wise, patient, relaxed, and able to participate joyfully with our youngsters and smile at their natural childishness. Group members urge me to "write about" the many insights we had come upon so that "other parents could share them."

I thought I could best do this by using the group context. This demonstrates what parents really do, think and say, and in some cases why. Through this material, I shall attempt to strip away your need to see yourself as a *supermom*, knowing and being all things to your child, and help you to accept yourself when you find out (over and over and over) that you are not.

As members of this society, young parents are usually very hard on themselves, expecting as if by magic to know just how to make the parental pathway a smooth one. Take for example the young mother with her first child, who read somewhere that newborn babies sleep about twenty hours a day. (The book actually said: "A very few babies may sleep as many as twenty hours a day.") What a holiday that would be—all the time in the world to get laundry, formula, housekeeping and even hair done. But apparently most newborns aren't aware of that possibility, and so prefer to sleep in small snatches whenever they happen to feel sleepy. A young mother fears that something may be wrong with her child, herself or both. Edgy because of her doubts and self-critical feelings, pressured and fatigued by her new duties and responsibilities, she is now in a position to start a parent-child battle. Parent-child tension has begun!

Cooling the Battle

Very young children exert a lot of power over their parents. Just watch any mother with a little one in the park, on the street or in the supermarket. That supermarket! Almost any toddler can make a wreck out of almost any mother there. By checkout time, both child and mother are tired, patience has worn thin, and tempers are tattered. Many mothers become embarrassed, ashamed of their inability to control their toddler's flailing arms clutching at anything within reach, or their quickly moving feet, carrying them beyond sight and sound.

It seems not to occur to parents that an ordinary marketing trip is too much for most little children. They often become tired and cranky long before Mommy is ready to leave; and she often does not do anything about it—for example, by doing the rest of her marketing another day. Inconvenient? Of course.

A mother and her young child were at the checkout in a supermarket. The child's hands strayed to the goodies temptingly displayed. Knowing from previous experience that these were not to be touched, the child looked inquiringly at her Mother. Mother didn't say a word but just looked down, very evenly. They stared at each other for maybe ten seconds, and then the child looked away. Little fingers caressed the chewing gum. Again the child looked up. Again Mother returned a long look. There was no frowning, no smiling—just looking. A third time the child looked up and after a few seconds, smiled at Mother. Mother smiled back, and kept looking. The child then grabbed Mother and gave her knees a big hug. Mother fondled the child and then asked her if she wanted to sit on the window seat while Mother checked out. The child seemed to have forgotten about the chewing gum and was content to sit down.

I don't have to describe what usually happens when mothers start to discipline their children about keeping their hands off things. This was an extraordinarily special piece of discipline. Everything was crystal clear to the child, and there had been no harsh words, ugly feelings or spanking. Children respond to such quiet discipline. However, if they are used to only harsh disciplinary measures, it is difficult for both parent and child to shift to a new method. Many tries are necessary before success is achieved. And it is achieved only when the mother can be very clearheaded as to the nature of the message. If the parent described above had smiled too early, the child might have taken the smile for a signal to grab the object. Angry or disapproving behavior could have upset the child. Subsequent behavior might then have been erratic and therefore conflict with well-being, which always depends upon Mommy's kind regard, and not upon her anger.

Why Does Mommy Get So Angry?

Well, there are all kinds of reasons why Mommy gets so angry when her child does something she considers wrong. First, she is angry because she believes she has not trained her child properly. He shouldn't go around picking up garbage from the street, should he? What kind of a mommy are you that your child picks up garbage?

Whether or not there is anyone else to observe all this is immaterial. You don't need anyone else to tell you that somehow you have failed if your child doesn't know any better. Then there's the making-more-work thing. If the paper is sticky and dirty, his hands will get sticky and dirty. He might wipe them on his jacket. The stickiness will pick up more dirt and you'll have to wash it off. If you're going anywhere, he'll arrive dirty.

So when the child does anything that can set such events in motion, Mommy gets so angry because of all these possibilities and not because the child has done something terribly wrong, or wrong at all. It's because, in her mind, *she* has done something terribly wrong. And it's terrible only in relation to an image she has of what a good mother should be. Her belief is that a "really good mother" would have a child who never did anything wrong. That he does, she feels, is a reflection of her own shortcomings for the world to see. She cannot tolerate that. She cannot yell at herself or slap herself. She doesn't even know what is motivating her feeling and behavior. So the little one "gets it." He's the bad one, not she. Sorry though it is, that is more acceptable for her.

The fact is that neither one is "bad." This badness exists only in relation to an inner, unrealistic standard of goodness. If this woman's image of mothering could be analyzed, we would find that in her fantasy view of motherhood, she should have a "good" child, not just occasionally, but in every single instance. Anything short of such a model isn't just a human lapse from perfection—it's a severe deficiency in *her*. You may say, "Ridiculous to that!" But if you do, then try to answer the question—"Why does Mommy get *so* angry when I do something wrong?"

Walking the Tight Rope

Don't think that I am saying that you should "go along with" your child every time she moves a muscle or opens her mouth. I only urge you to observe your child. Get to know her well. Read signals. Then you'll be in the best position to decide what you want to do. Your child cannot dictate your role, but she can make you aware of her needs if you will get to know your child.

If you can remember that your child is growing, and that he somehow feels that growing, you may be more sympathetic to erratic changes. He knows he's bigger, stronger, wiser, more informed. He may not be able to tell you this, but there's no doubt about it. He's ready for more experiences, more risks. He's not afraid of the things he wants to do. But you are. This is a big moment. Are you going to let your child grow without having to deal with and perhaps be infected by your anxiety? Are going to let the child move into each new month, watching carefully and restricting only those demands you have thoughtfully considered and decided that he is not ready for? You will be permitted to interfere to some extent without resentment. In fact, you will be permitted to interfere quite a lot. Children can be surprisingly reasonable. They have no natural instinct to fight you, but will if you provide the grounds.

You cannot, however, have it all your own way. You cannot restrict the child only to those experiences about which you have no anxiety, because these might possibly be too few for optimal growth. You will have to pluck up your courage and let her be. The toddler years are perhaps the most exciting for the parents who are frightened by the boldness of their children who rush to meet each day with joyous anticipation. In these years, you can see your child's personality begin to unfold, the manner of confrontation she will make to a wider world. Most children need help from their parents in these years. While children seem brash, impatient, all-knowing, they too have fears and trepidations. But if you are caught up in a struggle to keep them from growing, you will not notice the areas in which help is needed, and you will fail them.

This is a tight rope to walk. It is not wise to push a child beyond a comfortable level. Yet it is not helpful to overprotect and keep children from doing things they feel ready for.

Parents need to trust their children's judgment at times, for they often seem to know the limits of their abilities better than their parents do. They will not, therefore, usually push themselves beyond these limits. When your children want to do something new, ask how the decision has been reached. You'll find out some interesting things about your child.

Parenting doesn't come easy. It doesn't come free. It has to be worked out and given time, interest, energy, compassion for self and for the child. It requires watchfulness, attentiveness, willingness and loads of flexibility—not mushiness. Even with all this, mistakes will abound. It can be no other way. But successes will also abound, and for these, your child will be grateful. She won't tell you that now. You may have to wait ten or twenty years to hear it. But believe that she'll forget most of your "garden variety" goofs and wish that you could too, for guilt feeds on feelings of failure. Let them blow away and start each week anew.

Relax!

In case you are thinking that this mother business is too much for you, you must understand that you cannot be expected to be busy parenting twenty-four hours a day and seven days a week. Less time is fine, too, as long as it's spent on *quality* parenting. *How* you spend your time with your baby is the important thing, rather than the number of hours each day. The rest of the time, do some growing yourself. The growing parent is the more relaxed parent. And the relaxed parent is more likely to rear the happy child.

CREATING YOUR FAMILYPLACE

Does your family open Christmas presents on Christmas Eve? Or do they open them on Christmas morning? Do you go to your grandmother's home for Thanksgiving, or do your relatives come to your house for the turkey? Does your family talk over what you are going to do this summer, what courses you are going to take this fall, or do you mention it to your mom as you fly out the door on your way to school?

How do you like being in your family? Do you want a family just like it? Do you want your own home to feel, smell and look something like the homes you have grown up in? Do you want it more modern or more rustic? Do you want your home to have less furniture, more music, less light?

BECOMING A FAMILY

The minute you decide to become a parent through pregnancy, adoption or stepparenting, you are on your way to being a family. There are lots of definitions of family—but in this case, family means at least two generations living together. So a couple plus a child, or a single parent plus a child, or a single parent plus a friend, or relatives plus a child will make you a family.

"Family." It can sound like a hostile word, a comforting word, a scary word, a marvelous word, a romantic word, a depressing word, a hopeful word. It can sound both good and bad at different times. The image

127

you have of family, now, can change as you get closer to creating your own family.

There are all kinds of family structures, and some of them will be described here. No matter what kind of family you wind up with (many of you will be in different kinds of family structures in different years of your life), any kind of family structure can provide a place for growth—both parents' growth and childrens' growth. Your family can provide a place to learn and test out new ideas and experiences to grow on. The more you think about and plan your family life, the less it will "just happen" without your control. You and your husband can consciously create a lot of growth experiences. You can create the kind of familyplace that feels best for you.

CREATING YOUR FAMILYPLACE

No course or book or therapist can teach you as much about family life as you are learning simply by growing up in your own family. As you think about your own family, think about how each person in it communicates with the others: by joking, teasing, correcting, disciplining, listening, and all the many ways of communicating you have learned. Everyone in a family is connected to the others and affects each one of them. When someone is aggressive in the family, everyone else must respond to that aggression. When one person in the family is down, or high, or hopeful, or irritable, each member of the family is touched and somehow affected by those feelings.

Notice how your own family works. Think about how your parents are different because of you. Knowing your influence on the rest of the family helps you to see the kinds of things you can learn from your own children. As Dr. DeRosis points out in her article on growing children, they are not the only ones learning in a family. Children *teach* their parents, and parents learn and grow as their children grow.

FAMILY RULES

Some families are a better place for living than others. When each family member respects others in the family, and also values talking things out and listening to other points of view, the chances for a good place increase. It takes rules to express respect and privacy for others. Rules have to do with who cooks dinner, who cleans up, who does the laundry and when, and locks the door (bathroom or bedroom), who knocks on the door before entering, who can have friends overnight, who feeds the dog, pays the bills, gets the mail, changes the beds, picks up the clothes. In some families, rules, rather than family roles, determine who does what. And who does what determines how much time and privacy each person in the family has. Rules provide space for each family member rather than putting the necessary work all on the non-assertive family members.

The difficulty with making workable rules is that there are very few good examples to go by—especially if you are looking for families "that work." If you really get to know a family well, most seem to be in strife and stress. Families with teenagers have special difficulties because teens are just about to break out of their family and they often demand much more independence than their parents want to give. As a teenager, you will have plenty of chances to look at your own family and to see the changes going on there. Look, too, at those families you visit and see most often. Notice what it is you like and don't like about them, figuring out what would work best if you had a say. You *will* have a say in the family you create. And with that say, you will get the responsibility for following through on all your plans and ideas about your own familyplace.

FAMILY SURVIVAL

The family is a social system. It's the social unit where you learn the skills to live and enjoy other social systems, like your school, or dorm or work groups. If you think you have problems understanding the differences of others within your own immediate family, just imagine how those differences magnify when you consider people of other races, classes, and ethnic backgrounds, not to mention differences in age. Learning how to make peace, to negotiate, to manage your temper, to find comfort and happiness in your family, is excellent basic training for those things in the wider social systems outside. Whenever you're at your wit's end to figure out how on earth you can possibly survive in your own family, just think of the historical differences involved in the wars of the Arabs and Jews, who have actually signed a peace treaty. If they can pull that off, with compromise and negotiation skills, you can certainly help to make life in your family more peaceful.

FAMILY EXPECTATIONS

The traditional family structure consists of a mother, a father and children, living in one place. Some people still say that the father has to be the breadwinner and that the mother has to be at home with the children; but because most mothers are employed, we will call the traditional family structure a one- or two-career family.

There are all kinds of expectations and "shoulds" for a family. In order to create your own familyplace it's crucial to know what the world expects of you, so you'll be aware of the programming you're getting about how to be a family. Many of the family "shoulds" probably won't work for you—they work for very few people. You'll want to work out your own rules and rituals with your husband and children so that the rules are yours to have and to change—as they work best for you. Here are some expectations other couples have felt, and ways in which they dealt with family "shoulds."

MOTHER "SHOULD" STAY HOME

We learn through the media and children's books
that a family consists of two parents with the father out
working and the mother at home with the children. But
most mothers, for a variety of reasons, do not stay at
home. Sharon, 34, professionally employed and the
mother of a 10-month-old and a 5-year-old, puts it this
way:

> "Basically, it's very important to me to be con-
> tributing to our income. It was a strong feeling
> that evolved from beginning to think about earn-
> ing money while I was in college, and knowing
> that my mother had always contributed to our
> family. I'd known by the time we were ready to
> have kids that earning money for the family was
> really a strong feeling. We were married for five
> years before we had kids; I was twenty-nine for
> the first one. We took turns going to graduate
> school, with the other one paying for it. When I
> was pregnant with Chris I resented people asking
> me, 'When are you going to stop working?' It
> really got me angry."

Hilda, a 27-year-old youth worker and mother of
two toddlers, describes her choices for a two-career
family style:

> "I have put a lot of planning into childcare. Af-
> ter two months being home with the baby, I found
> I just couldn't do it. Over the summer it's great;
> my husband is home because he is a teacher and
> the family had a good time all summer. But in the
> fall when he went back to work and Todd started
> kindergarten and I was home, I started to go nuts
> after the second day with the baby. Well, you
> know, I had little projects to do, the garden,
> freezing, the house, but those things just drained
> my energy. You know, forgetting the economic
> situation and our goals in life, just thinking that if
> I had the choice to stay home or work, I just
> couldn't stay there."

Not *all* mothers want to go back to work when they have a baby. The expectation that mothers "should" stay home is borne out by many young women, especially if they aren't crazy about their work or if they've just started a career and haven't been promoted to a high level of responsibility and money. Staying home with the baby can be much more exciting and important than working all day in a typing pool. Many young mothers want to give full time to creating a familyplace for everyone in the family.

June Strong, a columnist for *These Times*, a Christian journal, writes about being at home with the children:

> "There is in woman a delightful response to color, sound, texture and form. When a woman hangs out the family laundry, she takes time to talk with the swallows teetering companionably upon her clothesline. When she gives the baby its morning bottle, she observes dark lashes feathered against creamy skin, the kissable curve of the cheek. When she kneads bread, she sees the beauty of her own capable, tanned hands as they work the dough into a satiny sphere. I would not want to have missed this for the dubious joys of having been general manager of the local department store, or of General Motors, for that matter."

Other young women see staying at home as a direct career stage in their life. Anna Marie, an early childhood specialist, tell us:

> "We waited to have children. I had been helping other people's children grow and develop as I worked with their parents for years. I just couldn't wait to have a baby of my own. When I finally got pregnant I wasn't about to let the baby go to some church basement for someone else to raise! I wanted an in-depth experience taking care of my baby. I wanted to be with other mothers and their children. I see childrearing as part of my education just as surely as if I went for an advanced degree in childcare. Actually, I don't believe that any-

thing could be better for me, with my career goals, then six to eight years of in-depth time with my own babies."

CHILDREN "SHOULD" COME FIRST

Some mothers want to put their children first, but they don't want to completely give up their careers. Many of these women decide to work parttime at home as their children permit them. They keep their time flexible, don't promise to make any quick deadlines, they work at a convenient pace for others in the family; these mothers are clear that the children always come first. Many women in the arts, craftswomen, some small-business women, women in cottage industries, sales workers in insurance and real estate, and professionals who can work at home as bookkeepers and accountants make a choice to do less paid work while their children are in school. But they do want to keep up with their particular work and not make a complete break from it. June Strong, author of *Mindy—Tintype of a Marriage*, describes one incident that makes life at home seem right for her:

"I had just settled myself this morning at the small desk in our bedroom to work on my manuscript. With pencils sharpened and a long yellow legal pad before me, I was still in the pondering state when a little voice outside the door asked, 'Would you have time to help me with these fractions, Mama?' . . . Pushing my writing notes aside, we tackled the offensive problems— reducing, borrowing, converting. It was slow going, and the young forehead wrinkled in confusion. Now and then a tear fell on the quarters and the halves which refused to make sense, but at last the page was done—the final row.

"'I think I've got it,' said the child, smiling proudly. 'I think so, too,' I replied, giving him a quick hug. I didn't add that tomorrow there'd be decimals and the percentages, then algebra, then geometry. Let him play, and be free in today's achievement.

"What about *me*? When would I be free? I knew the answer now. I had seen it in the child's relief, in his grateful eyes. I was free whenever I was wise enough to put first things first. The world is full of authors far better equipped to say the necessary things than I. But to these little people whom God has given me, I am necessary. No one can ever quite take my place. The demands they made upon me are part of my role as mother and should come ahead of every other interest."

Other mothers do not want to give up their careers. It's not just the media and books that dictate the expectations and "shoulds" for families. Employers do too. These expectations often hurt a mother's chances for being hired, and for promotion. For instance, when Karen, 32, a lawyer and mother of 2-, 3- and 7-year-olds, was asked if she had any family obligations that would make a fulltime, demanding job a problem, she said, "No, the children are a shared responsibility."

But the employer disagreed, and refused to hire Karen because of her three dependent children.

MOTHER "SHOULD" STAY HOME UNTIL THE KIDS ARE IN SCHOOL

Even if you plan a two-career family, the "should," for mothers, is that you will certainly stay home till the kids are in school, and "school" means fulltime school at 5 or 6 years old, not kindergarten or childcare. But here is how things turned out for Sheila, a 29-year-old social worker and mother of a 1- and a 3-year-old, whose husband also works.

"I had planned on taking off three months before coming back to work, but after one month the director called me and asked would I go to an urban health setting and help consult on a disabled children's project a few hours a week. When Jay was almost two months old, the daycare center staff called and said they had an opening for an infant, and if I wanted to hold it for a month

I'd have to pay for part of it. So I put him in three afternoons a week, and took on enough work to cover that during his second month. At three months I came back to work fulltime, and I've been working ever since."

MOTHERS "SHOULD" MAKE THE FAMILY

One of the most difficult expectations for mothers to overcome is that the Mother alone is responsible for a smooth-running family. The traditional homemaker concept sounds as if the mother were the only homemaker in the family. A more reasonable family style starts with the mother *and* father as homemakers. Then each child, as he or she can take it on, becomes a homemaker too. In that way, the whole family gets in on the cooking, the cleaning, the nurturing of each other, the fun, and the looking out for each other that makes the family a place of equal responsibility and equal input. Many women have worked toward getting their husbands equally involved with the familyplace too. Patricia, a 23-year-old medical student and mother of an 8-month-old, describes how her husband feels:

"My husband wants everybody to know that the word is out—a lot of fathers are in on caring for their babies. Every time I read an article about the disintegrating American family, it lays the guilt on women who are working. I get so damned angry because I feel the disintegration is because the fathers are out there working sixty or seventy hours a week, and going up some meaningless career ladder, instead of being at home with their growing children. For parents both to work less, and both be at home more, makes sense in our family and in many families of our friends."

MOTHERS "SHOULD NOT" COUNT ON FATHERS

Just as some fathers want to be in on childcare, not all husbands have a traditional view and want their wives to stay home. Not *all* husbands are that crazy about going out to work themselves. We usually think that the last thing a father would want to do is stay home and take care of the kids. Here is Marge, an insurance salesworker and mother of a 1- and a 3-year-old, and she tells us a different story:

"My husband really doesn't like working that much. He likes to do things around home, he is a real family man, and likes to be an active parent. He has none of those feelings that he has to make more money than any other man in order to be a real man, and it's just great—he is wonderful to live with. I was surprised when the baby was about a year old and Mark (my husband) was talking about his worry over paying the mortgage. I said, 'Well, you know, the house is fifty percent mine, too, and I feel as responsible for paying off the mortgage as you do.' And a couple of days later he said, 'You know, that's really a burden off my shoulders.' And I was surprised because I didn't even think I had to say that. I thought he knew. Because I had always felt that financial sharing was implicit in our relationship."

Getting rid of the family "shoulds" means that other alternatives and options have to be found for the family. Working out changes for the traditional expectations of a family is a very exciting place to be. If you want a familyplace with a husband and children, and you want to get rid of some of the expectations for a family that don't work for you, then your family has to be a comfortable place—a place to grow, a place to love and be loved, a place to try out new things. The more social changes you bring about, the more you are going to need a very comfortable familyplace!

YOU "SHOULD" BRING UP
YOUR CHILDREN JUST LIKE
YOU WERE BROUGHT UP

Another family expectation is that your own parents and relatives want you to be just exactly like they are. They will disapprove of a family style that is different from the way you were brought up. This "should" infers that your parents will give you so much flack to stay home with the baby that you would feel too guilty if you took a job. One of the things that people making changes in the world soon learn is that others get their clues about how to treat you from you. In other words, people learn about you by how *you* act, and what your attitudes are like about the choices you make. For example, if you leave your baby with a caregiver and act like you shouldn't be doing it, your relatives and family will get right in there and hassle you about it. But if you think it's the only family style for you, that it's the kind of familyplace you want to create, then you may get a reaction like Jeanine did. She's 23, a legal secretary and the mother of a 6-month- and a 2-year-old.

"My parents think it's great that our kids are in daycare and we are both working at what we want to do. We have had negative comments from uncles and aunts, things like, oh, 'The people you leave them with can't care half as much about them as you do,' which, you know, may not be true, but that really isn't the point anyway. It's surprising how fast your family learns not to give you flack when they see you doing things differently than they did."

CHANGES IN THE FAMILY

Just as your baby will change, you and your husband will change and go through developmental phases, too. You don't hear as much about parents changing, but you may have had some new ideas about growing parents after reading Dr. DeRosis' chapter in this book. As you grow, as your husband and your baby grow, your familyplace will become different. The everyday business of life changes according to when the baby is up during the night for feedings, when she has nap times, when she walks, when she goes to school, when she eats with you.

Your baby's development will bring changes to the family. You and your husband's changes of jobs, or shifts, or in the days you work—or another baby, or moving—make the familyplace different too.

Oftentimes someone in the family will resist change, and when that happens life is hard and everyone is tense. If you have always done things in a certain way, eaten at certain times, celebrated by going out for dinner, had a particular kind of birthday party, you may think that is the only way to do it. You may not want to change. If your husband has the same attitude, and wants to celebrate *his* way (which is different from yours) or eat at a different time, then of course you have to resolve how your new family is going to do things.

Some couples carefully plan change. If you notice, for example, that when you and your husband get home from work after the baby is picked up from childcare, everyone is at each other and really irritable, hungry and tired, you can change things. You can plan a change from the miserable way things are, and the rotten way you treat each other, to a comforting way to speak to each other, with an advance plan of what you will eat for dinner, so you don't have to think about it or ask each other what you want. You can smooth out the rough spots. Your family can bring about changes to make the familyplace a loving environment to come home to. Bringing about changes in your environment is a skill to develop that will determine what kind of place your familyplace will be. Not being afraid of change is a good place to start to cope.

As you read about the great variety of choices in childcare and family structure, including doing it all yourself, and as you look around at young mothers and fathers who are making choices, and older parents who have already made them, keep in mind that whatever their choices, it is always part of their career development. You learn the transferable skills repeated throughout *Be A Mother . . . and More*. Women staying at home fulltime without any paid work are learning problem-identification, problem-solving, and time-management every time they tend to a crying infant. Transferable skills are learned even while staying at home with the baby.

STEPPARENT FAMILIES

You can't have as many divorces and remarriages as we have in America today without coming up with a huge number of stepparents and stepchildren. A stepparent family has all the joys and hassles of a traditional family. Besides which, they have a few special problems *because* they are stepparents. Seeing problems coming is one way to cope with them. Here are some stepparent problems.

One of the difficulties about being a stepparent is that you don't have any legal status as parent with the child. No matter how much you love the stepchildren (or your husband loves his stepchildren), and no matter how much responsibility you take for them (and some mothers are the only parent taking care of the child), you still don't have any legal rights. Some stepparents adopt their stepchildren, if they are free to do that.

Another common problem is that the "other parent" can influence your new family a lot more than is good for your family. Jealousy and possessiveness come easily with the "other kid," the "other parents," the "other family," and patience and being responsible fly out the window.

It's also easy to treat the stepchild as a guest in the home rather than as a family member. That's hard on everyone, especially if there are other children in the family. It means that some kids are guests and some are family.

In some cases, the difficulties of being a stepparent are resolved because the adults who remarry have learned from their first marriages which things work

and which things don't work in a family. Talking with
other stepparents and reading some of the books for
stepparents can help you cope with the "wicked
stepmother" stories, and help make your familyplace a
place that you can create with your stepchildren. In
other words, knowing what some of the problems are is
part of the solution. For more help at being a stepparent:

Read *The Half Parent*, by Brenda Maddox, New
American Library, 1976.

Write for *Stepparent's Forum*. A newsletter for stepparents, out of print at this writing, but ask for the
back issues. Send $6.00 to Stepparents Forum, West-
mount, P.O. Box 4002, Montreal H3Z 2X3, Canada.

See *Stepparenting: New Families, Old Ties*. A film
by Henry and Marilyn Felt. It is twenty-five minutes
long, in color, and you can rent it for $35 from Poly-
morph Films, 331 Newbury St., Boston, Mass. 02115.

SINGLE-PARENT FAMILIES

Divorced mothers. Separated mothers. Never-mar-
ried mothers. Whatever the situation, there are a lot of
single mothers around (99.4 percent of all single
parents are female). And the number is growing. It is
happening so fast that the statistics are all out of date
and the schools and churches still act like it isn't so.
One of the reasons why it's such a hard problem to
cope with is because mothers don't see it coming. As
young women, they are not *planning* to end up being
financially and emotionally responsible for their own
children. It is all the harder to cope with because single
mothers are in shock. Young women are led to believe
that if they have a baby, if they only become a mother,
then they will be taken care of. Of that somehow, if a
baby is involved, things will shape up and take care of
themselves. New mothers say it's especially hard because, first of all, they always assumed that when they
became a mother they would be married.

THE UNEXPECTED

"I was on the pill, believe it or not. I went in for a regular checkup and the doctor said, 'You're pregnant.' I said, 'I can't be because I'm on the pill.' And he said, 'Well, you are, anyway.' It's not like what I'd thought it would be. Well, when I thought of having children I thought of being married, of course. But I don't know, I'm doing OK. When I got pregnant I didn't know what to expect. I didn't think about it. Whatever happened happened, you know? We were engaged to be married and I'd gone with him for three years—I was seventeen when I had the baby. Well, the thing is, we never discussed children, you know, and when I got pregnant I thought, well, we are going to get married anyway, so there is no problem. But, so he decided, well, he chickened out and he took off and so that was that. He went to Florida; he is there right now."—Cindy, 18 years old with a 6-months-old baby

A mother of a 7-year-old child who was never married adds: "It wasn't what I expected. I didn't think about it when I was nineteen years old. I never thought of my baby growing up and being a kid. I never thought I would be alone, that I would have to do it all myself. That I would have to work and he wouldn't have a father. I didn't know I would have the full responsibility. It's scary wondering if you're doing the right thing. There are a lot of guilt trips, like Jamie doesn't have a father and not taking time to spend with him, and you wonder what's going to happen to your child. Working and being both parents you worry a lot, and when you worry you don't move forward. It can be physically very tiring."—Wanita, 27, waitress

NOT SURE OF A BABY'S NEEDS

One of the most difficult problems for all young mothers is that they aren't sure about the developmental needs of the baby. They aren't sure that the way they are handling the baby is right. For single mothers it can be even worse because they are alone, with no other parent to give advice, take the baby for a while, reassure them that what they are doing is right. For example, a college student with a 2½-year-old, who was separated from her husband, said:

"All last winter there was no one to support me in the things I was doing with the baby. It was hard on both of us . . . Sometimes I feel that there are a lot of things I should do with her that I can't think of. It's a scary responsibility. I could do a hell of a lot to mess this kid up without even trying. When she was an infant it was a lot harder—it wasn't all the fantasy of having this beautiful infant. I wish I had been more aware of the fact that my relationship with my ex-husband was not always going to be the same. If I had it to do all over again I would have waited and had my baby after I had my head in one piece . . . I think the most important thing to having a baby is to have a settled space. What did me in the most was that we never had a home, or a settled place to be in. Being a mother is certainly not like the propaganda tells you it is. It certainly isn't all fun and games. I wish I knew more about child development so I could be sure that what I'm doing is right—or at least won't do any harm!"—JoAnn, 22 years old, college student, nurse's aid

Another mother who was worried about child development said: "I thought the baby would eat and sleep more like I do. I didn't think you had to get up so much at night. I can't get enough sleep when I'm up feeding the baby so many times, and

I didn't know that would happen."—Theresa, 17 years old, on welfare.

LOVE CHANGES

Not all, but many single mothers feel that the father of the baby is a problem. They especially wish they had known that their love for the father might change. As one single mother put it:

"I'm worried because my child doesn't have a constant father figure. His father is a bomb-out and has bombed out with Tom. He constantly lets Tom down about visiting, so I had to say no more visiting. People should realize this, that the father may not want to visit his kids. I wish I'd known that romantic love is not enough—it has to be a working relationship. I didn't even know what that was when I got married. If I had it to do all over again I would have stayed in school. I was growing. I wanted freedom and all that crap. I thought I could just go out there and fly!" —Sarah, 24, divorced with a 4-year-old, sales-clerk, waitress, bank teller, college student, on welfare

Another single mother, who lives with the father of her baby, says this about fathers and money:

"I wish I had known about what it was like not to have enough money, and I wish I had known that I would not always be in romantic love with the baby's father. I am a unit with the baby, and I worry about getting his father to move to where I will be going to graduate school next year. Being a mother and being rich is fine; poor and being a mother is not. The last year and a half I have been getting poorer."—Clare, 22 years old with a 3-year-old, college student living with the child's father

NO TIME, NO PATIENCE

For many single mothers, time is the most difficult issue. Most of them work or are fulltime students. They have to be solely responsible for childcare—and their work—and the laundry—and cooking—and shopping—and cleaning. The hassle is the everyday routine of too much to do and not enough energy left over for patience and a quiet time with the baby. For example, a single mother of three children describes what it's like:

"Hard work—a lot of hard work. I love 'em all (a 7-, a 4- and a 2-year-old). I wish they were someone else's so I could love them more. No one ever told me about the fact that there would be two or three loads of laundry a day or other related things—time I would rather be using to read the children a story or play. I wish I had known about colic before I was a mother. I found out that the first four months I wasn't able to enjoy my baby because he was screaming all of the time. A three-year-old with an earache has to be held for hours because it takes time for the medicine to work. You don't just pick up a three-year-old and tell him the pain is going to be gone in an hour. You're crying with them. The frustration, the fulltime, long-term commitment to raising a child—you have to set aside twenty years of your life. Having a baby is nothing like what I thought it would be. You see people with babies on TV—bouncing a baby on their knee and no conflict, but in real life it's a hassle when they fight and when they all want my time. There's three of them and they get lumped together as 'children.' If I'm holding the baby and the other two are fighting I know it's related, but I can't put him down because they're fighting. It drains me!"—Hannah, 29, divorced, waitress

And Sarah, the mother of a 4-year-old, who is now going to college, agrees with Hannah.

"I've gotten out of class at five thirty to have Tom waiting at the door with the daycare teacher. He's grumpy after being at daycare. I realized I had to make dinner. He was in the tub and I was just sitting down on the living-room floor and bawling like a baby. It felt like the roof was caving in. Welfare isn't really enough—there is never enough time nor money to go on."—Sarah, divorced, on welfare, going to college

A 30-year-old single mother of two summarizes the way most single mothers feel:

"I think that being a single parent is a lousy way to go. It's too draining on your energy. You don't have the freedom of leading the social life of an adult. Also, the children need a social life too. The child is a life—a whole life, not just a mouth to feed. It's not something you can say you don't like anymore and stop doing it."—Jean, divorced, teacher

MONEY

A single mother needs friends and money, just like the rest of us. But the stress of being the only one caring for a baby, and being totally responsible, puts even more pressure on a mother's need for friends and money.

Let's start with money. Look at the jobs the women cited earlier in this chapter are doing, or have been doing: salesclerk, waitress, bank teller, teacher, nurse's aid and student. Some are on welfare. Like so many women, they are in the "pink collar ghetto," and that is exactly where the money is the lowest you can earn—in so-called "women's work." Partly because they are young and female, and partly because they didn't take advantage of educational opportunities that would have helped get them into better paying careers, and partly because they were thinking about marriage and motherhood instead of marriage and motherhood *and making money*, and partly because it all just happened, most single mothers are in a bad place to earn good money.

No matter what your situation is now—whether you're a high school or college student with time for planning and making good career decisions, or a pregnant student who doesn't have as many choices, or a young mother who may or may not be single—start thinking and planning to set your career goals by reading "Is There Life After Motherhood," beginning on page 153. The first chapter in this section, "Money: Making and Managing It," ties into career-skills assessment and educational and career decisions. It's wonderful to be a mother—if you have the time and money and relationships that will provide you with the energy and patience to be the kind of mother you want for your baby. But it's awful to be a mother *without* the time, the money, the friends and the energy that it takes to be a mother. Even with a loving partner, being a mother has its ups and downs. Without that partner, motherhood can bring your life to a virtual standstill, demanding a lot more human effort and struggle than you have to give.

Here is the story of one mother receiving welfare:

Barbara Cunningham says she can't afford to work. The 30-year-old, recently divorced mother of two has never been unemployed for more than three to four weeks at a time in the past three years. She has worked as a secretary for the county state's attorney and several law firms. In 1975, she became the first woman auxiliary state police trooper to obtain full law-enforcement powers, handling her own Snowmobile patrol.

Spirited and independent, she takes pride in her appearance and in providing for her family. But she can't continue to meet her expenses at her current wage. The reason?

"Childcare is my highest expense. It costs me sixty-five dollars a week," she said.

Recently Ms. Cunningham took her case before a hearing officer of the State Department of Social and Rehabilitative Services (SRS) to protest a decrease last

July in the amount of money she receives for daycare for her children. Her plea fell upon deaf ears.

She was told by the hearing officer of the state Human Services Board that her appeal should be to the Legislature, which determines the guidelines for distributing welfare and SRS funds, and not to the department, which merely enforces the regulations.

But Ms. Cunningham went to the hearing, as she put it, "not to fight, but to make a point."

"I don't understand how you can turn me down when I ask for help with baby-sitting expenses, yet you would pay me more (welfare) if I stayed home. I'm trying to be independent and not collect anything from the state, and I'm not happy with the answer."

Ms. Cunningham has been unemployed for the past two weeks. Before that time she was making $160 a week. Because one of her children is pre-school age, she qualifies for welfare assistance under the Aid to Needy Families with Children program. Her alternative is to take a job she has been offered beginning in October and continue to draw assistance for childcare from SRS.

But because of her income level, SRS guidelines require that she pay 30 percent of her childcare costs, an expense she says she cannot afford.

"Three years ago I knew what it was like to feel no self-worth." she said, recalling the days just after her separation when she collected welfare, and would dress down in jeans to look inconspicuous as she cashed in food stamps.

"Now I'm responsible for two kids. I'd like someone to say, 'This is a valid point and let's do a study,' work together, rather than taking the negative attitude that nothing can be done about the regulations.

"I bet they would save money. But the children are my main concern."

FRIENDS

The first way out of the crunch is through friends. Friends provide you with a support group. Look for other mothers who share your single-mother experience. One of the first places to look, if your friends are not in the same boat, is to Parents Without Partners, the international, non-profit educational organization devoted to the interests of single parents. They have chapters all over the world, and a national headquarters, with magazines and articles for you no matter where you live.

Finding others to share the single mother's experiences in providing her baby's needs can make the developmental problems of a 4-month-, an 18-month-old or 5-year-old much less difficult. You will learn what other babies of similar age are like, and how other single mothers manage.

One of the dangers for single mothers who feel alone and unsure of themselves—afraid they can't make ends meet, afraid they won't have enough time and energy for the kind of care they want to give their baby—is that their babies will pick up the same fears and insecurities the mothers have. In addition to getting rid of energy-draining fears for your own survival, it is necessary for you also to be an example to your baby. As you learn survival skills with a baby on your own, you also will be teaching your child that solutions are possible. No matter how difficult the family situation may appear at any time, you will want your child to learn that there is always a way to improve it, that there is always hope.

YOUR MOVE

Taking the initiative for getting out from under this tough problem is a difficult skill for young women to learn. You have been brought up to believe that *someone else* will always help, or take over, or take the initiative. When you are in a stressful place, it's hard to go against the things you learned so well about being a woman. But if you wait for help as a single mother, you will have a long wait. Start helping yourself right away by learning to take the initiative to get the support that you need:

READ! *Momma: The Sourcebook for Single Mothers,* New American Library 1976,

$3.95; *Tea for One: A Survival Booklist for Parents Without Partners* (available from Parents Without Partners, address below).

WRITE!   Parents Without Partners, 7910 Woodmont Avenue, Washington, D.C. 20014, and ask for the local chapter nearest you.

JOIN!   A group of single mothers, parents working on child-development issues, an adult education class, a woman's group, and/or Parents Without Partners.

SHARE!   Your experiences with other single mothers, find them at school, daycare centers, at work and in groups as above.

CALL!   A friend or an acquaintance to talk about an activity you can share with or without your children—this week!

TRADITIONAL PARENTS

Say you've been married for one, or two, or three, or four years. You're part of a happy couple. Both of you have been creating your familyplace. In addition, each of you has been working outside your marriage. Now you have a baby and your life is complete. Your family is what it "should" be. You've got everything. There is great comfort in a traditional family. No matter who works where, or who brings in the money, if there are two parents and children, you don't have to explain your family structure to the outside world. Everyone understands where you are: It's the ideal.

The myth of the ideal family is sometimes hard for new parents to live up to. They often think something is wrong with *them* if family life doesn't feel as great as it sounded. Making the change from being a couple to being new parents is an experience that needs the support of friends, just as the single parent and stepparent need support from their friends.

One difficulty with being traditional parents is that it's easy to get stuck in rigid "mother" and "father" roles, even when they don't work for you. Some new parents decide before the baby arrives that they don't want the traditional roles, where the mother does all of the childcare (or finds someone else to do it), and the father does none. But when the baby actually arrives, they often are surprised at how hard it is to work out who does what and why. They are surprised that it's not as easy as they thought to work things out with a new baby—a completely dependent human being—in their life. Changing the traditional roles, even when both parents agree on the changes, can bring stress to everyone. A baby in your life *does* tie you down. Deciding which parent will be tied down when, and how often either of you can have the house, gets into the nitty-gritty of what makes life feel good or not feel good with the new baby in your life.

Another difficulty is not being able to get out and meet new people with different experiences. Most people think the perfect family "should" be able to care for themselves. As if they don't ever need other people. When others don't come up with solutions for being isolated, it's easy to get stuck at home. One mother, who is trying to break out of the "our whole family does everything together" idea, finds it almost impossible for her 2-year-old and herself to go off to the beach with other families because they are never invited. She explains: "My husband doesn't like to go to the beach with Adam and me. We would like to take a picnic and spend the day at the beach with other families. They never ask us because they know my husband doesn't like to go to the beach. I am trying to think of some way to get invited, or to ask a family to go with us, but I'm afraid they will think there is something wrong with our family."

Traditional parents can learn to develop and grow beyond the "ideal" myth. They can plan to be helpful and friendly with people outside their marriage, which will keep them from feeling so isolated that they have to solve all of their problems alone. They can also plan changes within, changes in who does what with whom, so that everyone doesn't have to do the same things at the same time.

Traditional parents can look forward to a life-style

that can be fulfilling. Holiday rituals and the shared history and longterm commitment to other family members can be a comforting environment for growth. Economically, traditional parents who are not supporting children and spouses from previous marriages are better off whether or not both parents work outside. Watching their children grow from birth till they leave home can bring a shared closeness, and increasing pleasure and satisfaction, to traditional parents.

A FAMILYPLACE

No matter what the structure, a family is the place where you learn to live with others. A place where you teach your baby to live with others. How your child learns to live with others is central to his everyday enjoyment of life. How he learns to live with others is central to how he feels about himself.

A familyplace is where children learn to be sensitive to others, to laugh with others, to notice the special needs of others, to be assertive or aggressive. To exploit or help others. To manipulate or to negotiate and compromise. Children first learn to respect others, and to give the clues about how they expect others to look at and treat them, in the familyplace.

A familyplace is worth plenty of time and thought and patience because it's the strength and center of your life—the place where you go out from, the place you always return to, the place where you explore living with others. It's a personal-relations learning center. There's no other institution that socializes babies and young children for their expected role as the family does. When it's *your* familyplace we are talking about, that means it's *your* children who are getting shaped by the climate you have helped to create. The more everyone in the family is in on the creation of the familyplace, the more they can take responsibility for it and the more they can get from it.

Expect more than survival in your familyplace. Expect an abundance of life with love. Whatever you and your husband can come up with and achieve, is what you are teaching your baby is possible. A family woman and a family man deserve a loving familyplace. So does a family child.

IS THERE LIFE AFTER MOTHER-HOOD?

Of course there is! There is even life *with* motherhood that has little to do with the mother part. If you are at home with your baby, you are learning new skills and acquiring new interests as you care for your baby. If you are a mother who works part- or fulltime, you have a separate work life from your child. Your life in community service, or in making money, or in sports, or in the arts, can be integrated with motherhood, but it is separate from being a mother. As your children grow older and more independent, your life focuses less and less on motherhood until your children leave home. Planning for your life after motherhood assures you of many options for a life of abundance, choices that you have been designing all along—during the years you were directly into motherhood.

In "Life Career Skills," beginning on page 172, Ellen Wallach develops a process to help you identify where you are now and where you want to go. She has designed a series of 9 exercises for you to do on your own, or in a class, or in a group. If you aren't in a

formal group, Wallach recommends that you get a
friend to share the exercises with you. You will learn
how to assess your skills, which skills you enjoy and
value most, how to develop a master career exploration
list and how to use this list. The outcome of this
process puts together what you know about yourself,
and shows you how to use that information to further
explore your career possibilities.

Learning to understand money, learning how to
assess your skills, and developing the strategy and
goals for your life plan will best help you to be a
mother . . . and more.

MONEY: MAKING AND MANAGING IT

MAKING IT

How much time do you spend thinking about making money now? About making money in the future? Isn't it odd that in a country with all the things we have to buy, and all the advertising about how you need material goods in order to be happy, and with all the focus on spending, that half the population isn't even encouraged to think seriously about making money? Do you have a brother? Or a boyfriend? Talk to them about making money. After a short time you will probably hear that they just naturally assume that they will make money to support themselves plus others. The "others" will mean their family, including wife and children. Now talk to your girlfriends and your sisters about making money. You may hear many of them say that, if all goes well, they will have somebody else making money for them. Unless, of course, something awful happens—like they don't get married. Or something happens to their husband. Take a look at the adult women you know and notice their jobs. Ask them about their work and if they prepared in school for their present job. If you go along with the idea that someone else will financially support you, then you will live your life right now, while you're in school, as if school is an end in itself rather than a place where you *could* be preparing to make money. You, like your brothers, could be learning the necessary skills to empower you to have career choices.

155

Chances are, your mother, aunts and many of their friends are working to make money. As you look at women you know, notice what they are doing to make that money. Notice what happens to the young woman who has a baby and no husband to support her. Notice the young woman who used to be in school getting ready for a career in engineering, or nursing, or business administration, when she suddenly had to quit school to have her baby. What is she doing now about money? How would her life be different if she could make money right now? Enough money to support herself and their children.

If you begin to include making money in your thinking, as you plan for other things in your life, you will soon see that there is a lot to think about. The notions of career development, career goals, financial credit, college, childcare, training programs, jobs and unemployment are all part of it.

MEN MAKE MORE

The first thing you should know about making money is that women still make much less than men do. For the same work. And besides that, women don't usually *get* the same work. They usually get jobs in places where most women work, and places where most women work means a lot less money. As a waitress, you will make less than a bartender. You will make less in a beauty parlor than a male hair stylist. You will make less in nursing—even with a Ph.D.—than a doctor. You will make less in teaching than in engineering. So the first thing to learn about making money is that *the money is where the men are.* If you keep in mind that a female college graduate makes the same amount of money as a male high school drop-out (about $9,000 a year in 1980), then you will see where you are and where you have to go. To support your children. To be financially responsible for your own baby.

HOME WITH THE BABY

If there is any choice at all, a young mother and father should try to work it out to be with their child most of the time until he is 2 or 3. After 3 the whole world is different for a youngster. For one thing, on the practical side, there are a lot more and better nursery schools than daycare centers. The older child is ready for the more independent activities that are offered in nursery school. Many professional women, who don't want to interrupt their careers while their babies are infants, work only parttime until their children are 3. Working parttime and finding someone *good* to be with your baby 1 or 2 days a week, or 2 or 3 hours a day, is much easier than finding someone good for a 40-hour week. If you are married, working parttime is usually possible. But it is very difficult for the single mother to earn enough money and to be with her baby that much, especially if she doesn't have a highly flexible or high-paying job. And how many young mothers do you know with high-paying or flexible jobs?

PARTTIME OPPORTUNITIES

If you decide to have two or more babies, and you decide to stay home with them at least parttime until they are 3, that may mean that you will take 5 years or more to do it. Five years of child-rearing counts as part of your career development as much as it counts toward the start you are giving your children in their development toward being loving, independent people. Your school preparation and your work experience make a big difference in what you can be doing during those 5 years of parenting. If you wait and have your children in your early thirties, as many women who have been promoted to responsible and flexible jobs do, then you will have time to work out ways that will give you time to be with your baby when he arrives. If you have your baby during or right after college, and you are trained to teach, or to be in sales work or in banking, and have little work experience, it's hard to get parttime work. Except for saleswork. Selling real estate, insurance or new cars 'on commission can be well-paying work for parttime workers, and in fact thousands and thousands of salespeople work parttime. Often the work is at night or on weekends when you might find it easier to get help with the baby.

If you have a baby when you're halfway through college, and you're majoring in early childhood education or history or English literature, you will need quite an imagination *and* a lot of luck to find some way to make money and be at home with your baby. On the other hand, if you are a technical student and learning a skill in your high school right now, such as welding, printing, accounting, or how to be an X-ray technician, then there is a very good possibility of getting a parttime job with your specific skill. But a general course in high school, community college or college, and an unplanned pregnancy, really cuts down on your chances for work. It cuts down on your chances for making the money you will need to help support your baby.

DEVELOPING SKILLS

The time to work on your skills for earning money is *now*. Now, while you're still in school and can do most about it. You often have the same education opportunities that your brothers and boyfriends have, but perhaps you don't feel the need of using these opportunities in the same way. You have been so well programmed to think that you will be financially taken care of, maybe, that you aren't as serious as your brothers are about making money. Many educators aren't serious about your need to make money either. They expect you to remain at home, and they often treat the years you spend with your children as if they don't count. But, in fact, *everything you do is part of your career development*. If you take 1 or 5 or 10 or 15 years off to rear a family, you are still developing skills that count toward a paying job. Many women in their forties, who are going back to work after being at home, are taking classes to learn how to assess their personal skills developed while working at home. Money management, time management, decision-making, persuasion skills, problem solving, peacemaking skills, are all part of the everyday skills used by every person raising a family. In addition, the community work you do develops other skills in group work, leadership and fund-raising. You don't have to wait until you are 40 to start thinking about the skills you are learning. Start right now, as a student, to plan your career goals. Rather than thinking that you'll be out of the job market, or that you'll have an interrupted career plan, keep in mind that everything you do is a place to learn skills. Skills you learn at home, in volunteer work in the community, with children, with your hobbies and sports, can all be transferred to paid employment later. Start seeing yourself as one who is learning transferable skills—no matter what your activities are. Be confident about your skills developed at home and in the community, because you *know* you can use these skills to make money. You, just like everyone else, will want to make money because you will need it. And, besides that, making money feels good.

Using our skills and interests to make money gives us the control we need over our lives—control that leads to our independence and confidence, which is the foundation for a mature personality. Ask all the women and men who have already earned more money than they need—or inherited money, or are being supported by their parents, spouses or welfare—why they work. You will find that meaningful work for pay is a strong force in feeling good about yourself. Even Jackie Kennedy Onassis chose to work because she knew she had unique interests and abilities to offer the publishing world where she worked . . . and she also knows that it feels good to be paid for that contribution.

And just as important as making money is *managing* money.

MANAGING MONEY

It may help you to manage your money if you know that *no one* ever has enough of it. Sometimes you may think that when you are earning *more*, the time will have come when you can take care of all your needs and wants. The truth is that the more you make, the more needs and necessities you will have.

Money is for spending. But the way you spend your money either brings you closer to, or takes you further away from, all your hopes, your ambitions and your aspirations.

Managing money is more than a question of dollars and cents. For example, a money plan ties into both time and energy when you are deciding about the time you can spend being with your baby as opposed to the time and energy you must spend financially supporting your baby.

You may decide that your time and energy and services at home would be a better financial plan than the cash you can bring in by working outside. Just because you aren't actually bringing in the money doesn't mean that you aren't in on the money management. A family is a financial-based arrangement. Both partners have to be in on the responsibility for managing the finances, regardless of who makes how much. The more you agree with your husband about the kinds of things you will spend money for, the amount you will save, the ways you can avoid spending money, the kinds of things each of you can do at home instead of hiring it done, the better your money management will go. The more money-talk you can pull off with the man you are going to marry *before* you get into a financial crunch, the easier your money-talk will be later. Chances are, the amount of money you bring in compared to what your husband brings in will change during your married years, but the amount of responsibility you take for money management should *not* change. Equal responsibility has to be taken by both partners for a money-management plan to work.

Learning to manage money is possible for everyone.

Basic skills are involved. Money management starts with a plan.

PLANNING SKILLS

1. Know exactly what you have coming in—that means your take-home pay, or allowance, or both. If it's a paycheck, remember the deductions of Social Security (which buys your retirement income, disability income, survivors' benefits, and Medicare after age 65), group insurance, retirement income or pension plan and taxes. Figure it out in terms of monthly income.

2. Know exactly what your fixed expenses are—rent or mortgage, travel expenses to work, installment payments on a car, television and any other purchases, insurance, taxes, membership dues, tuition at school. Also contributions, garbage collection, cable TV, paper delivery, magazine subscriptions. Also savings.

3. Know exactly what you can spend for day-to-day living—what you have left after the fixed expenses for food, clothes, drinks, recreation, gifts, supplies, electricity and telephone bills.

4. Know exactly how you will budget the day-to-day living expenses.

Money-management plans never work if you have to account for every penny. If you know that a given plan is impossible—change your plan. Know that you must have a personal allowance that does not have to be accounted for to others you live with. You can agree with your partner or parents on the *amount* of the personal allowance, but you should also agree that everyone has a right to that amount without accounting for it to anyone else—even if it's as little as $3.00 a week! Your plan will work if you expect an actively changing budget and reevaluate as you go along. A budget should be flexible; if it doesn't work, change it!

SHOPPING SKILLS

All money-management plans will have a better chance for success, regardless of the amount of money you have to spend, if you can sharpen your shopping skills. Here are some ways to do that:

1. Make a list; stick to it. Curb your impulse-buying and don't buy items nearest the cash register.

2. Eat before you go grocery shopping—so that you aren't hungry for everything!

3. Compare before you buy. Either shop around or, easier yet, use a Sears or Ward's catalog to get an idea of which prices apply to what quality.

4. Shop for specials and items on sale, but be sure it *is* a sale—and not a promotion.

5. Don't let charge accounts trick you into thinking you are staying within your budget. Remember: the finance charge is 18 percent and going up for charge accounts—and that's more than you are earning in your savings account at 5½ percent.

6. Buy the quality that you need.

7. Read labels before you buy so you know what you are getting.

8. Shop at stores that you can trust.

Most important while shopping, ask yourself if you really need it. From the Council for Family Financial Education, here is a quiz that offers some help on that crucial decision:

TO BUY OR NOT TO BUY

1. Do you really need this item? . . . . Yes   No
2. Is the price reasonable? . . . . Yes   No
3. Is this the best time to buy the item? . . . . Yes   No
4. If this is a bargain, is it a current model (if that matters to you)? . . Yes   No
5. If "on sale," is the price a true sale price? . . . . Yes   No
6. Are you sure no less expensive items can be substituted? . . . . . . Yes   No
7. Are you sure there are no major disadvantages? . . . . Yes   No
8. If excessive in price, will it truly satisfy an inner need? (If not excessive, just check "yes") . . . . . . Yes   No

9. Have you checked and researched
   the item? .... Yes   No
10. Do you know the retailer's repu-
    tation? .... Yes   No
11. Does this retailer offer any special
    services with the item? .... Yes   No
    Score your answers as follows:
    9 to 11 yeses—buy the product.
    6 to 8 yeses—think again.
    Fewer than 6 yeses—forget it.

HOW MUCH DEBT CAN YOU AFFORD?

Everyone who buys, has to deal with credit. Just as
there are guidelines for developing your planning and
buying skills, there are guidelines for developing your
credit skills. There are basic amounts of money that
are safe to borrow, and if you borrow over that you
can't hope to have a stable money-management plan.
As you start buying, keep these three credit rules in
mind:

1. Never owe more than 20 percent of your annual
take-home pay—with the exception of a mortgage. If
you take home $10,000, a safe debt is $2,000.

2. Never owe more than 10 percent of the amount
that you can pay per month for the next eighteen
months. If your take-home is $1,000 per month, you
can pay $100 per month. In 18 months this would be
$1,800—your debt limit for the year.

3. Never owe more than one-third of your income
that you have left *after* you pay your basic living expenses.

According to some money-management specialists,
the first debt you owe is to yourself. Saving money is
hard, especially when you don't have any idea of how
much you are expected to save. Skills that everyone
needs are how-to-save-money skills.

SAVING SKILLS

How much money should you save, and how much
money do you have to save before you're "safe," or in

a "good money position?" Here are two good guidelines:

1. Include in your savings total an emergency fund equal to at least two months' income, to cover the costs of unexpected illness, repairs, moving expenses.

2. As a starter, put aside 5 percent of your total monthly income for savings, and save more from there as you can afford it.

There they are: planning, shopping, credit and saving skills. That's all there is to it.

MONEY MANAGEMENT NEEDS FOR COLLEGE STUDENTS

Most things you read about money management assume you are earning money, receiving a paycheck. But many of you reading this book will be students getting an allowance from home. If you are a student, you may want to consider some of the following points that are special:

1. Consider your allowance your paycheck. It deserves the respect and care you give a check when you are working. If you are on scholarship or from an affluent home, if you have a lot or a little, the principles of good money management are all the same.

2. Plan the amount of your allowance with your parents before you leave home. Be as realistic as you can. Be sure to include cleaning costs, shoe repair, the ever-rising price of gas for your car, new jeans, Coke, beer and coffee money. Don't go by what your older brother or younger sister spends—it's *your* plan. Really think it out with your parents beforehand.

3. Deposit your allowance in a checking account and draw on it only when you need to. A pocketful of money goes faster than money that takes a little effort to get.

4. Start a savings account for your tuition, rent, and big expenses that don't come as often. Try to save some money each week—no matter how little—to get in the practice of saving, for the sake of the investment and future income for you.

5. Give yourself a break: Don't plan your money

down to the last Coke or cup of coffee. Give yourself some leeway or you will feel so constricted you'll be tempted to forget the whole thing.

6. If you aren't sure where your money is going, keep an exact record for a day, or even a few days. Be like the smoke-enders who are told not to cut down on cigarettes until they *notice* and are aware when they smoke. Notice and be aware when you spend money.

7. Buy wisely. Refer to the "To Buy or Not To Buy" questions on page 162. When you can, buy special sales and economy sizes. Just as important, don't buy. Or don't always go out to eat. It's easier to keep the money you have by not spending it than to find new money!

8. If your plan doesn't seem to work, don't be afraid to make changes. Your parents can be reasonable, and if you have put this much effort into budgeting (buying wisely, recording where your money goes, having a money-management plan) they are more likely to listen and renegotiate with you.

THE BEST THINGS IN LIFE ARE FREE?

After working on a money-management plan, and learning exactly where the money comes from and where it goes, the major events of life can hit you like dynamite—and send you and your plan flying in all directions. Marriage and inflation and babies are at the top of the dynamite list.

HOW MUCH DOES IT COST TO GET MARRIED?

The average bride (and according to *Bride's Magazine,* four out of every five young brides will choose a traditional, formal wedding—and that includes a diamond ring) will spend more than $3,000 for wedding goods and services. Every year over $14 billion are spent on the bridal market, most of that in the furniture and home-furnishings market, and more than $1 billion in the honeymoon market.

In order to keep down the getting-married expenses,

you will want to know how to figure out what the actual costs are before you have to pay for them. There are a lot of hidden costs—the wedding dress, for example, does not cost as much as the miscellaneous items such as flowers, music and photographs. The minimum you can spend for a church wedding, with only a few guests, is around $500, to cover the costs of a dress, invitations, flowers, a reception and refreshments. If the reception is in a hotel of course, you can get an exact per-person figure, which will include the food, beverages, services, music, flowers, cake, bartender, coatroom, taxes and tips. Then there are the bridesmaid's gifts, special transportation to the wedding and to the reception, hairdressing costs and sometimes the cost of a tent, awnings and dance floor.

As you figure your costs, the point to remember is to get all of the estimates, and then plan for unexpected expenses that will be billed to you after the wedding. No matter what the occasion, there are always ways to save and better ways to manage your money. Each occasion gives you a chance to use your money-management skills. Sylvia Porter has some ideas about saving on your wedding and honeymoon in *Sylvia Porter's Complete Money Book*. For example, she suggests that you choose a home wedding, make the reception simple and serve a wine or champagne punch rather than have an open bar. A cocktail buffet rather than a sit-down dinner is cheaper, and often people find the more informal setting more fun. Consider the service of a professional catering service, which provides a package deal where you will be very clear about the costs. Choose a wedding dress that you can use for other occasions. For your honeymoon, work with travel agents on a package plan. Packages are by far the best bargains and the further you plan ahead, the more you can take advantage of money-saving offers on flying.

HOW MUCH DOES IT COST TO HAVE A BABY?

Weddings often lead to life's next major expenses. And it's not true that the best things in life are free—

when you start to figure how much your new baby will cost! The Health Insurance Institute estimates that a baby costs close to $2,000—and that figure only gets you through the first week at home, not counting twins or complications.

The biggest expense is the hospital care. In 1979 a single day in a short-term general hospital cost $140—and the average stay for maternity cases is about 4 days. Delivery- and nursery-room charges and other items count as extra expenses.

The next biggest costs are the supplies, clothes, and furniture for the baby, which can total more than $500 for the first baby. This includes a basic wardrobe for the baby, bathing equipment, baby furniture and nursery items.

The next item is medical care. The obstetrician's services are usually paid for at a package price. The average fee in a small city in a teaching hospital is $400. Some fees, especially in cities, can go up to $1,-000. Plus there is the pediatrician's new-born-baby fee while the baby is in the hospital. And last is the cost of a typical maternity wardrobe, which averages $250 to $300 for the first baby, according to the Health Insurance Institute. The best plan is to check the list that the Health Insurance Institute used to get their figures (given below) with your local hospital and stores (or a Sears or Ward's catalog), to find out what these costs are right now, in your local area. Maybe you can get one of your school classes, or friends, to share the research, going through the list together to find out local costs. If you know what the exact figures are, you can save by getting insurance coverage ahead of time, by borrowing baby furniture and maternity clothes, by staying in the hospital no longer than necessary, and by comparing doctor and hospital or clinic fees. Find out for yourself—how much does it cost to have a baby?

NEW-BABY COST CHECKLIST

HOSPITAL AND MEDICAL CARE	COST IN YOUR AREA
4 days' hospitalization	_____
Delivery-room charge	_____

Nursery charge, 4 days   _____

Circumcision setup charge   _____

Obstetrician's fees   _____

Circumcision fee   _____

Pediatrician's newborn care   _____

TOTAL   _____

BABY'S WARDROBE

Shirts (4 to 6)

Gowns (3 to 4)   _____

Sleeping bags (1 to 2)   _____

Stretch coveralls (3 to 4)   _____

Receiving blankets (4 to 6)   _____

Diapers (4 to 6)   _____

   (if using diaper service)   _____

Diaper pins   _____

Sweater or shawl   _____

Waterproof panties (4)   _____

Booties and socks   _____

Bunting   _____

TOTAL   _____

NURSERY ITEMS

6 fitted crib sheets

4 waterproof sheets   _____

5 waterproof pads   _____

3 crib blankets   _____

1 blanket sleeper   _____

Comforter or quilt   _____

1 mattress pad   _____

Bassinet or carrying basket   _____

Crib   _____

Crib mattress   _____

Crib bumper   _____

Diaper pail   _____

Portable baby seat   _____

Wicker changer with drawers   _____

Nursery lamp   _____

Vaporizer   _____

Baby carriage   _____

TOTAL   _____

FEEDING EQUIPMENT

8 to 12 8-oz. nursers; 2 to 4 4-oz. nursers; extra nipples, caps; disposable nurser kit, sterilizer kit, or separate formula utensils; bottle and nipple brush   _____

Hotplate   _____

Bottle warmer   _____

2 to 3 bibs   _____

TOTAL   _____

BATH ITEMS

Bath table or tub   _____

4 washcloths, 2 towels   _____

Lotion   _____

Baby oil   _____

Cream   _____

Powder   _____

Sterile cotton and swabs   _____

Baby shampoo   _____

Bathing cream or liquid   _____

Petroleum jelly   _____

TOTAL   _____

MISCELLANEOUS

Baby vitamins   _____

Sweater set   _____

30 disposable diapers   _____

Baby-care book   _____

Diaper bag   _____

Brush and comb   _____

Crib mobile   _____

Rectal thermometer   _____

Baby scissors   _____

Car bed or seat   _____

Birth announcements   _____

TOTAL   _____

MATERNITY CLOTHES

2 dresses   _____

2 skirts   _____

4 tops   _____

2 pants   _____

a slip   _____

3 bras   _____

4 panties   _____

TOTAL   _____

TOTALS

Hospital and medical care   _____

Baby's wardrobe   _____

Nursery items   _____

Feeding equipment   _____

Bath items   _____

Miscellaneous   _____

Maternity clothes   _____

GRAND TOTAL   _____

After you've figured out the cost of the newborn baby, it's time to figure out what comes next.

HOW MUCH DOES IT COST TO BRING UP THE BABY?

The U.S. Department of Agriculture says that it costs 15 to 17 percent of a family's income to bring up one child. If your income is $10,000 a year, you can plan on spending $1,500 to $1,700 for the baby's clothes and food, extra rent for a larger place, the medical and other expenses of child rearing. This cost assumes no childcare fees, which will be extra.

No matter who cares for the baby, it costs money. You will want to think ahead about all of your choices. Even if you or the father stays home and cares for the baby, the lost paid-work experience, lost earnings, and lost work seniority are hidden costs that must also be counted.

Infant care is another expense for the two-career family, for students, or for single mothers. A national survey of typical costs for group infant care by the Child Care Information Exchange showed that there are no "typical" costs. Reported costs ranged from $25 to $121 per week for full-day, five-day-a-week group infant care. One infant-care center in a city of 80,000 in the northeast charges $50 a week. The center is run by the Visiting Nurses' Association; it has the maximum professional staff necessary, excellent facilities and is based on psychologically sound principles of childcare. In other words, it's the best you can get. But $50 a week for 50 weeks a year adds $2,500 to your budget. How much money do you have to earn to *bring home* $2,500? Again, there are other hidden costs in everything. It's not just the money you bring home that counts in a job. If you are a graduate student, if you are just starting out in business, if you are in a training apprenticeship, the money you make is really not as important as the investment you are making in your future. You have to compare more than the present take-home pay you are making (unless you're in a dead-end job) to find out if the $2,500 is worth the price of infant childcare.

There are options other than daycare centers. (See "What Are the Childcare Options?" page 50.) The point to be made here is that major events in life have to be planned for financially. Getting married, having a baby and rearing a child are easier to cope with if you see them coming. If you see their money, and time, and commitment costs as well as the hopes they promise to fulfill.

LIFE CAREER SKILLS: WHAT ARE YOU GOING TO BE WHEN YOU GROW UP?

by Ellen J. Wallach

It always seemed to happen the same way. The relatives would reappear after years of absence, pinch my cheek, tell me how much I'd grown (as if they expected me to remain four feet forever!), and then ask, "What are you going to be when you grow up, Ellen?"

Sound familiar? Recently, this same scene occurred in our house with my five-year-old daughter, Cathy, at the hurting end of the pinch. Her answer was obviously well thought out and spoken with confidence:

"I'm going to live in South California because it doesn't snow like it does here in Boston. I'm going to marry a man who goes to work in the morning, comes home for lunch, and stays and plays with me all afternoon. I'm going to make arts and crafts and sell them in my own store."

It all sounds so wonderful, so clear, so simple! It's easy to be sure of yourself when you are five years old. How much more complicated life becomes as we get older! We become increasingly aware of our expanding options as we learn more about ourselves and our world. The more alternatives we see, the more confused we become, and the more difficult it is to make a choice among them. And yet, we feel tremendous pressure to make "the right decision" about our lives.

There is no *one* "right decision." Today's young women have many more options than their mothers did twenty years ago. When your mother was your age she believed in "happily ever after." She would grow up, perhaps go to college, perhaps go to work, with the unspoken and unquestioned understanding that her paid employment would end as soon as the first child was born.

The world is changing. More and more women are in the workplace because they need to be. They need the money to support themselves and their children. Each individual makes her own choice. You will have choices to make at each decision point in your life. If you choose motherhood, the arrival of your first child will cause a reconsideration of previous decisions and a careful appraisal of the new options open to you:

- working fulltime
- working parttime
- staying at home with your child for some months or years

The important issue for mothers to remember when making a choice is that there is a new life to consider, and you still have only 24 hours each day to balance your life among:

- child and home responsibilities
- other family members
- friends, leisure, recreation
- alone time
- volunteer work and education
- paid employment

As a balloon can only expand so far before it bursts, you, too, cannot keep adding new roles and responsibilities and keep the old ones unchanged. You cannot have more than 24 hours a day to work—either at home or elsewhere. You must weigh your priorities and make decisions about what you can do and where you may need to give up some responsibilities, or get some help in fulfilling them. For example, if you choose to be a fulltime paid employee when your baby is two, you will need to find another person to help provide childcare while you are away from home.

You may choose to work parttime. Perhaps you can negotiate a schedule which is mutually convenient to both you and your employer. Perhaps you can arrange flexible hours or work at home. Be creative and don't be afraid to negotiate for what you want! If you decide to stop working for 2 or 3 years, what effect will this decision have on your career?

Every experience counts. We learn from everything we do. Taking care of a home and children is part of your career development too. Think of all the skills and abilities involved in the performace of these responsibilities: child-raising, financial planning, bookkeeping, comparative shopping, cooking, managing time, planning and scheduling, interior decoration—to name a few. Among these skills would be decision making, creativity, planning, organization, quick-thinking, patience, diplomacy, persuasion, time management and more. Being home can provide you with time to take another look at your career and reevaluate your goals. Being home can also allow you time to explore new opportunities for learning:

- Consider volunteering in a leadership role for a church or school organization, if you are considering working in management.
- Consider volunteering to do publicity for the local acting company if you are considering advertising or public-relations work.
- Consider taking some courses in areas that are new for you at a local community college, YWCA, center for continuing and adult education.
- Consider subscribing to professional magazines and journals, or joining a professional association for a career which interests you as a new possibility.

The list is really endless. Be creative. You never need to stop learning, growing, and developing your abilities and experiences. Helping your baby grow and learn may be your work for now. You can watch your own skills grow toward paid work later.

This chapter will help you identify where you are now and where you want to go. It will provide exercises and techniques which will assist you in:

- assessing your skills and abilities
- determining which skills you most enjoy using and which need further development and practice
- describing your values, work satisfaction, interests, and preferred people-and-work environments
- developing a master career exploration list
- investigating, through the use of written and people resources, these career options
- thinking creatively about yourself and your career

The exercises in this chapter follow a logical sequence. They build on each other; they form a process. Begin at the beginning. Keep all your work together in a notebook just for your career exploration.

The exercises are not difficult, but they will require time and thought. The more reflection and effort you give to this task, the greater the rewards in increased self-awareness. The more you know about yourself, the easier it will be to make career decisions and the better your chances of being happy with them. Self-awareness is the key to making the best decisions for you. So, answer as honestly as you can. No one else will see your work; you are doing it for your own benefit. And, if you change your mind about the answers to any of the exercises, you can always go back and change them. Nothing you write must be forever. Everything is subject to change, as you change.

What Can You Do?

What do you think? Would you rather hire Joan as a have? Joan loves to fix things. Anytime anything is broken around the house, she takes it apart to see how it works and whether she can fix it. She'll watch the mechanics fix the car and ask thousands of questions. Joan is taking a business curriculum in high school, but finds typing and shorthand boring.

What do you think? Would you rather hire Joan as a secretary or as a trainee in a telephone-repair program? The point is that life experiences teach us as much about our skills as school experiences do.

By looking at various life experiences we can determine our abilities. These abilities—aptitudes, talents, competencies—are our personal strengths. They are called our TRANSFERABLE SKILLS because we use them over and over again in many different situations and in a variety of activities. As we examine our life experiences, patterns of transferable skills emerge. These patterns will consist of the skills we use most often. We then choose which of our transferable skills we most enjoyed using. On the basis of past experience we will be better able to predict which skills we will most enjoy using in the future. We will also become aware of skills that we may wish to further develop and practice.

Anne graduated from a commercial high school 7 years ago and was a secretary for 2 years before she married and stopped working to stay home with her two children. She enjoys making many of her own clothes and has become proficient at operating a sewing machine. One of the accomplishments of which she is most proud is her ability to fix things around the

Anne's Transferable Skills	Secretary	Sewer	Homemaker	Handywoman
eye-hand coordination	X	X	X	X
manual dexterity	X	X	X	X
attention to detail	X	X	X	X
ability to follow directions/procedures	X	X	recipes X	X
understanding of how machines operate	X	X	X	X
problem solving	X	X	X	X

house. She wants to go back to work, but not in an office. What can she do? What skills does she have?

A variety of skills can be found in all of the experiences mentioned above: secretary, sewer, homemaker and handywoman.

You can probably find more examples of transferable skills. If so, add them in the extra spaces provided.

Different occupations can be looked at from a "skills" point of view, too. If we examine a job, we find it is composed of many tasks. The performance of each of these tasks requires a particular set of skills. Two seemingly unrelated jobs—surgeon and car mechanic—have several transferable skills in common:

Transferable Skills	Surgeon	Car mechanic	
eye-hand coordination	X	X	
manual dexterity	X	X	
attention to detail	X	X	
ability to follow directions/procedures	X	X	
understanding of how machines operate	X	X	
diagnostic ability	X	X	

Can you find others? Again, add them if you wish.

Now, let's return to Anne's problem. What can she do? What would you suggest? We already have some idea of her skills. They match those of both the surgeon and the car mechanic. They also can be used in many other technical jobs: lathe operator, welder, and medical laboratory technician, to name three. Her choice will be determined by her interests, values and goals, and her ability, desire and opportunity to pursue further education.

Earlier we described TRANSFERABLE SKILLS as abilities, aptitudes, competencies—our personal strengths. We often take for granted those abilities which are our strongest. Perhaps it is because they seem to come naturally, effortlessly, without pain. It is always easier to see how many "talents" our friends have. It is more difficult to find our own strengths. What are your TRANSFERABLE SKILLS? When people say, "You're so good at _____" or "You really should be a _____," what are they telling you? What skills of yours are they acknowledging?

Just for fun, take a piece of notebook paper and write down your transferable skills. Do your best; don't be modest; give yourself the benefit of the doubt. Now let's proceed to a more systematic method of getting at these skills, and see how accurate and complete your skills list is when compared to the list you develop as a result of these exercises.

EXERCISE 1: Choosing an Achievement.

The best way to find our TRANSFERABLE SKILLS is to analyze the experiences in our life which we consider:

- an achievement
- an accomplishment
- a satisfying experience, or
- an experience of which you are proud or feel really good about

Think of one life experience which qualifies. It doesn't matter what the rest of the world thinks. In fact, you may be the only one aware of what you did! If you feel proud, if you feel it is an achievement or an accomplishment, it counts! None of us have as yet won a Nobel Prize, been nominated for an Oscar, or been given a standing ovation in the Houston Astrodome! *You* are the only person to judge what is important and meaningful in your life. If you feel good inside, *it counts!*

Take a piece of notebook paper and write the title of the experience you chose at the top. Think about what you did. Write it down in the order that it happened. Write the story as though you were telling it to a young child—simply and clearly. Start at the beginning and tell it as it happened. You don't need to write complete sentences or worry about grammar or punctuation. The important thing is to remember as much as possible about all the things you did to make the experience happen. If you don't like to write, jot down some key words of the story and number them in the order that they happened. Or, outline your story. Or, tell it into a tape recorder or to a friend who can write it down for you. Again, keep asking yourself, "What did I do to make this happen?"

In our society we place a high value on modesty. We are not expected to tell everyone how wonderful we really are! Well, this is not the time for shyness and modesty. Be brave, be bold, tell the world just how terrific you are! Allow yourself the pleasure of enjoying the wonderful life experience that you have made happen.

The importance of this is reflection. As times passes, we sometimes forget all the small things that were part of an experience. By writing everything down, your mind will focus on this experience and keep recalling new aspects of it. Your recollection will be more complete.

EXERCISE 2: Finding Transferable Skills.

My grandmother's birthday is May 1. The year that I was fifteen it was April 15 when I realized that I didn't have enough money to buy Grandma something special. I only had $4.00, but I knew that the gift would be very special to Grandma if it was something that I made for her myself. I thought a lot about it and looked in some stores. I decided to embroider a sheet and pillow case with a flower design from a pattern I found in the same store. Two weeks later at the party, when the presents were opened, mine was the most appreciated. Everyone "oohed" and "ahed." I felt so proud! On page 180 is an example of my skills chart for the story above.

Take out a piece of notebook paper and draw a skills chart like the one shown on the next page. Enter

My Skills	Grandma's present			
using my fingers	X			
eye/hand coordination	X			
asking instructions in store	X			
showing attention to detail	X			
budgeting	X			
knowing what Grandma would like	X			
following instructions	X			
completing task in time	X			

the title of your experience in the first slanted space. Think about your experience. What did you do to make it happen? What TRANSFERABLE SKILLS did you use? Think about each skill and try to choose words which demonstrate specific skills. What word or words best describe what you did? You may not have used skills in any particular category. If not, go on to the next one. Each time you will be writing skill words in the lefthand spaces of your chart and "X"ing the appropriate box under the title of your experience.

EXERCISE 3: Completing Your Skills Chart.

In order to complete your skills chart, you will need to think of four other life experiences that you are proud of or consider an achievement or an accomplishment. Most people have trouble thinking of four experiences immediately. You may even be saying to yourself, "I don't have four more achievements in my life." Perhaps I can help by having you focus your thoughts. Remember, think about your whole life, not just this past year. Also, think of your life in pieces:

- school and educational experiences
- volunteer experiences
- leisure and hobby experiences
- paid and unpaid work experiences
- family and friend experiences

School and educational experiences: Were you a member of the school band? Did you write an outstanding paper? Did you have a part in the school play? Design a poster? Write for the newspaper? What clubs did you belong to? Were you on an athletic team?

Volunteer experiences: Did you volunteer in a hospital? Did you collect money for charity? Did you run a carnival or other fund-raising activity?

Leisure and hobby experiences: How did you spend your free time? Do you teach Sunday School? Ski? Swim? Go camping? Repair cars? Sew?

Paid and unpaid work experiences: Did you ever earn money? Selling? Babysitting? Delivering newspapers? Doing lawn work? What about non-paid work experiences? Did you paint your room? Decorate it? Bake a special cake for a friend: Just because no one pays you for your efforts doesn't mean it isn't work! Think about your unpaid experiences.

Family and friend experiences: Did you do something special for someone you love, like my present for my grandmother? Did you help someone out of a jam? What special experiences have you had with your family and friends?

Don't be concerned about which category things belong in. The categories overlap. The goal is to reflect on your life and remember your accomplishments and satisfying experiences.

This exercise may take a few days to complete. It's hard to remember everything at once. Write down as much as you can. Then show your chart to your parents, a friend, a brother or sister. Perhaps they can refresh your memory and help you add to your list. Then leave it on your desk in your room and glance at it each day. You will probably find that you will be remembering more and more as the days go by. Your mind will be working on remembering your life experiences even though you may not be consciously thinking about it. And don't worry if you can't think of experiences in each category. They are just there to help you remember.

Try to develop a list of more than four accomplishments. The more you write down, the more you'll think of. The longer your list, the more choice you'll have in choosing four for your skills chart. Again, you may not think of everything at one sitting. Leave it for a few days. Eventually you'll be surprised at how many things you've done in your life that you're proud of.

Once you feel that your list is fairly complete, you can begin to select four more to add to your skills chart. You might choose the accomplishments of which you are most proud. Or, you might choose four which represent different aspects of your personality: creative, physical, emotional, intellectual. Or, you may decide to select one experience from different school grade levels. The decision is yours. There is no right or wrong. If you can't decide on four, that's OK. There is nothing magical about four. It can be five, six or seven. In fact, once you get started, you may want to add new ones and eliminate some of your original choices.

Enter the titles of your four experiences in the slanted spaces of your skills chart. For each title you enter, check to see if any of the skill words you have chosen for preceeding experiences are relevant. If so, "X" in the appropriate box. Add any other skill words that best represent what you did to make each experience happen. Use the skill categories at the end of the chapter to help focus your skills assessment.

As you analyze each experience for the skills you used, you should begin to see patterns, skills you use over and over in different circumstances. These are your strongest TRANSFERABLE SKILLS.

As we discussed earlier, modesty is considered a great attribute in our society. In order to lessen its effects, I suggest you show your skills chart to someone who may be more impartial about you than you are about yourself, perhaps a parent, a friend or a teacher. Let them look over your skills chart and see if you've left anything out. Describe one or two of your experiences and see if they can add any skills to your list.

Look back at the list of transferable skills you made before completing these exercises. How well did you do? How complete was your list? How many more skills do you now have and, more important, BELIEVE you have? If you are like most people, your list of skills has grown as a result of completing the exercises.

EXERCISE 4: Enjoyable Skills.

Each of us has many transferable skills, but we don't enjoy using them all equally. This exercise will help you select which skills you *most enjoy* using. For example, when I purchased the supplies to make my grandmother's gift, I had to show attention to detail. I included this skill on my skills chart. However, I do not *enjoy* showing attention to detail.

Look again at your skills chart, starting with your first experience. Consider each skill which you used to make this experience happen. For this experience, did you enjoy using it? Sometimes we enjoy using a skill at one time and not at another. So, focus on this first experience before continuing to the next. If, in fact, you enjoyed using this skill, color the appropriate box with a bright colored pencil or marker.

For each experience, look at each skill you "X"'d and consider it, using *enjoyment* as the only criterion for your coloring.

You now have a colorful array of boxes representing the skills you have used that you most enjoy. Which of these skills would you most like to build into your future work?

EXERCISE 5: Transferable Skills for Future Use.

You have many skills which you enjoy using, but which would you like to build into your future work? On the basis of *enjoyment only*, which skill clusters would you most like to include in your future work? It isn't important how much experience you have in using these skills in the past. Choose the three or four clusters you would like to use in the future. Write each of these "most liked" cluster titles on a separate 3 × 5 card. Looks at your cards. Try to put them in order, from most-liked (1), next-liked (2), and so on. Once you have made some decisions about the clusters, number them 1,2,3 and 4. If you absolutely must include a 5th, feel free. There is nothing special about the number I have chosen, I am merely pushing you to make choices and think further about what you most enjoy doing.

Look at your most important skill cluster, "most important to be included in your future work." Which skills on your skills chart are included in this cluster? Look at these skill words and, again, try to order them in some way from most-liked to least-liked. Write your words in the order that you have selected on the card with the cluster title. Reflect on your life in terms of this skill cluster. Which three life experiences most indicate that you possess these skills? You may use incidents which you have included before, or you may think of new ones. It doesn't matter. Choose the two or three best. Write a sentence describing each on the back of the card. By thinking about your life in terms of using certain skills, you should see even more clearly that you possess these skills. You may also find skill areas that you enjoy, but which need more practice or experience. Complete this exercise for the three or four skill clusters that you have selected as "most desirable" for future work.

You should now have a good idea of which skills you would like to use in the future. You should also know which skill areas are of interest to you and which you would like to develop.

By looking at your past experiences, you have found your most enjoyable skill areas. We will now explore, again benefitting from life experiences, where you would like to use these skills:

• what kinds of people you like to be with
• what kinds of environments you like to be in

- what kinds of things and ideas are of interest to you
- what in your world is important to you, of value to you

EXERCISE 6: Life Experience Worksheet.

Take a piece of notebook paper and graph it as indicated below: Be sure to leave room to write experiences under each heading.

	like	dislike	learn
School/educational _____ _____ _____			
Volunteer _____ _____ _____			
Leisure/hobby _____ _____ _____			
Paid/unpaid work _____ _____ _____			
Family/friend _____ _____ _____			

Under each category, jot down experiences which you feel the strongest about, either liking or disliking. It doesn't matter whether you feel positively or negatively toward the experience, just that the feeling is strong!

Then look at the first activity you listed under school/educational. Think about it carefully. What did you *like* about it? What did you *dislike* about it? Try to be as specific as possible. For example:

School/educational	Like	Dislike
Collecting money	—being outdoors	—talking to strangers
door-to-door so	—walking	—asking for money
school band could go to state	—working as part of a team	—being refused, rejected
championships	—keeping records of contributions	—doing it alone

What did you learn from this experience? I learned that if I went with others I wouldn't be so lonely and the rejection wouldn't hurt so badly.

As you can see, for almost every activity there will be *likes, dislikes* and *learning.* By choosing the ones you feel most strongly about, you will discover your strongest likes and dislikes.

Try to be as specific as possible. Did you like or dislike working with people, numbers, things, machines? Did you like or dislike being with children, older people, people your own age? What kind of people do you like or dislike being with—artistic, intellectual, social, athletic? Do you like or dislike being alone or with others? What kinds of environments do you like and dislike—clean or dirty, noisy or quiet, indoor or outdoor? Think about the teachers, parents, bosses and other authority people in your life: What do you like and dislike about them?

What's important to you? Do you find that you keep volunteering for activities that have to do with cleaning up the environment? Are you always fixing things and interested in how things work? Do you find that you like to be with other people and help them; do you volunteer to teach or assist people in some way? The more specific you are about your like-and-dislike answers, the clearer the patterns that you will see in relation to your interests, the kinds of people you like to be with, and the kinds of environments you enjoy. You should also get some idea of how you respond to authority; what kind of supervision you like while you are working.

You may also see the outlines of some life goals. If something is really important to you, you will probably work toward that goal and make decisions to further this effort consistently. If you volunteered to work at the town dump sorting cans and bottles for recycling, if you were active in getting people to sign conservation petitions, if you spend a lot of time talking to friends about the environment, if you discuss the issue of sonic booms and gas emissions with your parents, if you find articles about conservation particularly fascinating . . . you can begin to see patterns of interests.

Look at your worksheet. Jot down some patterns that your answers indicate, on the back. Look again. What else do the choices that you have made in your life say about you, your likes, dislikes, values and interests? Show your worksheet to your friends, teachers, counselors, parents, anyone who knows you well. Ask them to help you find the patterns. Write what you have learned on the back of the worksheet.

EXERCISE 7: Work Values and Satisfactions.

Each of us will find different satisfactions in working. Each of us will work for different reasons (once you have made enough money, whatever "enough" means to you, to support yourself and others). What's important to you? What will motivate you to work?

Get a copy of the "Help Wanted" section from a Sunday newspaper. Although you will find advertisements for employment every day in the paper, Sunday's paper contains the largest number of ads each week. If you live in a small town or rural area, buy a Sunday newspaper from the largest city near your home. Read every advertisement carefully. Cut out the ones that you find attractive in some way, even if you don't know anything about the position being advertised and you don't have the education to qualify for it. Tape each ad you like onto a piece of notebook paper.

When you've finished, look at each advertisement and ask yourself: "What about this job did I find attractive?" Be as specific as possible. Write down next to each ad as many attractive features as you can find. Some of this information will reinforce what you have already learned, from the *LIFE EXPERIENCES* worksheet. But what else can you learn about your work values and satisfactions?

What are the most important rewards and satisfactions you will need to get from your career? Will you need a lot of money, a lot of power? Do you need to interact with many people, perform a variety of tasks, have a high status position, have a lot of vacation time or good health benefits? Do you need to be able to structure your own time? What's important to you? Write your answers on the back of the paper. Try to number them in order of importance. If push comes to shove, what's most important, next most, and so on.

If you have faithfully followed the instructions and exercises in this chapter, you have probably learned a great deal about yourself. You have organized the information about your life and have reflected upon your past experiences and choices. You should have clearer ideas about the skills which you enjoy using, your interests, the people and work environments you prefer, and your values and work satisfactions. Now that you have this information, where do we go from here?

EXERCISE 8: Who Are You? Putting It All Together.

You have examined some of the pieces of the puzzle that is *you*, individually. Draw a diagram like the one below. Let's put all the information together.

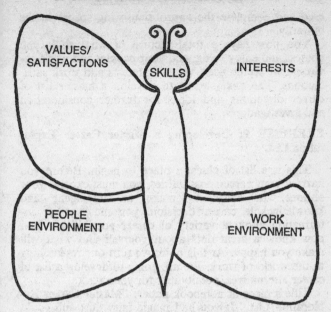

To complete the body of the butterfly, you will need the skill cards from Exercise 5. Copy the cluster titles and the individual skill words for each cluster, starting with card #1, in the body of the butterfly. You may need to draw the body chubbier to fit it all in! You do not need to copy the experiences you listed on the back of the cards.

Next, look at your answers to Exercise 6: "Life Experience Worksheet." On the back of the worksheet you wrote your likes, dislikes and learning patterns. What do you know about yourself? What kinds of people do you like to work with? What kind of environment would you like to work in? Any other important information you learned about yourself? Complete the answers to these questions in the appropriate wing spaces. Complete as much of your butterfly as possible, using the answers to Exercise 6.

Next look at your work values and satisfactions, Exercise 7. Again, look at the patterns you have uncovered and complete the appropriate wing spaces in the butterfly.

You now have a total picture of what skills you possess and enjoy using, and your people- and work-environment preferences, values, interests and work satisfactions. The next step is to develop a master list of career directions and ideas for further consideration and investigation.

EXERCISE 9: Developing a Master Career Exploration List.

This is a list of clues; a place to begin. Before you narrow your career possibilities, you must expand your options. In order to make an intelligent and knowledgeable career decision, you must gather information about a variety of career possibilities. You now know a great deal about yourself and what will make you happy. At this point we turn our researching to the world of work. We are going to develop a list of career alternatives, possibilities for your work.

Title a piece of notebook paper: "Master Career Exploration List." If you had magic fairy dust and could go——pooooof!, what would you like to be? Forget the educational requirements or money needed to make it happen. Think of two or three things, or more. What would you be if you could be anything: Remember, now is the time to include *every* possibility. We will eliminate later.

Next, think of what other people have told you—your parents, teachers, counselors, friends. Have they ever said. "You really ought to be a _____?" You may not like the idea, but include it anyway. That way, if you reject it later, you will have done so after first researching the possibility and deciding, with good reason, that it isn't for you.

So, although parents and others often exert tremendous pressure on you to follow a particular career direction, don't dismiss these ideas immediately. Research them; investigate these possibilities. You may find that they were good suggestions for you, or you may decide to eliminate them from your list. If you do choose to reject these suggestions after researching them, you will have many good reasons why they are not the best choices for you. You will have good information for explaining why you decided against them. You will have accurate, well thought out reasons to back up your decisions.

Most of the ways we learn about careers do not provide accurate, impartial information. Aunt Ernestine is a nurse and hates it; you'll never be a nurse, right? The other ways we learn about careers—through television and movies, say—are equally biased. Perhaps you thought you'd like to be a big-city detective because you saw *Policewoman* on television. One person may find the job appealing because Pepper Anderson had a lot of power, or she was physically attractive, or she helped people when they needed it, or she got a great deal of respect, or the work was dangerous or exciting, or whatever. You rarely see her doing the hours of paperwork that is typical for police work; you rarely see her working on many cases at one time, also truer to reality.

Take your butterfly to a friend, a parent, a school counselor, or a teacher. Explain what you have learned about yourself and see if they can add ideas to your list.

Another way of developing your list is by reading information about different careers. Read J.S. Mitchell's *I Can Be Anything: Careers and Colleges for Young Women*, a book written just for women which describes jobs available to them. And to learn about trade, technical, and business jobs, read *The Work Book: A Guide to Skilled Jobs*. Some schools have extensive resource centers with a variety of books, filmstrips, tape cassettes, and even computerized career information. Perhaps you are lucky enough to have such information available to you. If your high school doesn't have a career resource center, try a local college. Your library is another good place to begin your search. Resource librarians are information detectives. They can get you practically anything you want. And if they can't get it through inter-library loan, they'll surely tell you how to find it and where. Ask your librarian for the *Occupational Outlook Handbook*. This

huge paperback book is published every other year by
the Department of Labor and is a basic resource for
career information. It contains information about over
800 careers. Browse through it!

The very best way to expand your list, and also to
learn about different careers at the same time, is by
talking to people. Look at the first career idea on your
list. Think of where you can find someone who is doing
that job so that you can discuss their work. Nervous,
shy? Take a friend who is also interested in the career
with you to interview the person. Don't know anyone
who does that job? Don't know where to find them?
Here's an illustration:

Suppose I know that:

- I like working with my hands
- I like using my senses: examining, observing
- I like logical thinking: diagnosing
- I like working with animals, particularly horses
- I like working outdoors

I may have any number of career ideas on my list, including:

- veterinarian, for horses
- ranch or range manager
- horse trainer, thoroughbreds, rodeo horses, circus
  horses
- jockey
- farmer

The first career on my list is "veterinarian, for
horses." I could begin by speaking with veterinarians
who provide health care for pets, such as dogs, cats,
parakeets. The first place to look would be the Yellow
Pages of your telephone directory. Finding someone
who specializes in caring for horses might prove more
difficult (depending upon where in the United States
you live). Where do I begin?

1. The Yellow Pages, my 1978 Boston area book,
did not list any veterinarians who specialized in horses.
There were hospitals, clinics and kennels, but nothing
especially for horses. Following the "Veterinarian" list-
ings was "Veterinarians' Equipment and Supplies."

Listed here was Horsemens' Equine Sales and Service, Inc., in Pawtucket, Rhode Island. A letter to this company, which services veterinarians with equine equipment, might yield the names of horse specialists. I also looked under "Equine" and found nothing.

I might try calling a nearby vet and asking her for the name of a specialist. I might also ask for the name of the local professional association to which veterinarians might belong. A call to the president of the organization, again requesting the name of a horse specialist, might prove helpful.

2. Ask friends, relatives, teachers, guidance counselors for names of people in your town who own a horse. If someone owns a horse, they will probably have the name of a vet who is experienced in treating it.

3. Again, in the Yellow Pages, under "Horses." I found "Horse Breeders, Horse Boarding and Rental (see Riding Academies; Stables), Horse Dealers, Horse Feed (see Feed Dealers), Horse Training, Horse Transporting, Horse-Saddles-for-Hire (see Riding Academies; Stables)." There were lots of leads. It makes sense that any place that has horses or sells horse supplies would know the name of a vet specializing in horse care.

4. Where else would I find horses? The mounted police? Farms, ranches, riding clubs, racetracks? Even circuses and zoos. Even if a zoo didn't have a horse, the vet there would be used to working with large animals as opposed to pets. Even if you live in the middle of a city, there are horses around, if you look carefully and creatively enough for them.

Think of this search as an adventure or a mystery novel. You are using the clues and creatively putting together the pieces to find people to speak with about their career. Your career topic probably won't be as difficult as the one I've chosen as an example. You can probably get a good start by just talking to people who you already know:

• parents, friends, relatives
• teachers, counselors

- people in your church or temple
- people in groups to which your parents belong: Chamber of Commerce, fraternal organizations, political groups, unions
- local business people: the shoemaker, cleaner, grocery store manager, dentist, doctor, etc.

Look around your community. Everyone is a potential resource!

Well, you now have names of people who do the job you are considering. What do you do with them? Call them. Tell them you are interested in learning more about what a _____ does, you are considering pursuing it as a career. You'd like to talk with them, at their convenience, for thirty minutes or so. Could you make an appointment. (Ask specifically for a short period of time, otherwise the person may be afraid that you will prevent them from doing their work by taking up too much time. My own and my students' experience, however, has been that once people get involved talking about their work, they'll just go on and on and forget about the time!)

You may be thinking, "Why would they want to talk with me? What's in it for them?" The answer is that most people enjoy talking about what they know best—themselves and their work. Oh, some people will be abrupt or rude because they are short of time or having a bad day, but you will find that most people will be cordial and happy to speak with you. In fact, I bet you'll be amazed at how many people will spend time with you and share information with you, once you get started!

You have an appointment. What do you say when you get there? Explain why you are there and try to get the person to start talking about their work. Perhaps the following suggestions will be helpful:

1. How did you get into this career?
2. What did you perceive before you got into it? Is it different? How?
3. What do you like *most* about your work?
4. What do you like *least* about your work?
5. Why did you choose this type of work?

6. What are the greatest pressures, strains, anxieties about your work?

7. What special problems might someone new to the job have in adjusting to it?

8. Would you make the same career choice again? Why?

9. Where else, besides the environment in which you work, could someone perform your work?

10. Are there related careers?

At the end of the interview, always ask the following question:

11. Is there anyone else you know who also does your kind of work and who might be willing to speak with me?

May I use your name when I call?

The last part of the question is very important. It is always easier to get an appointment with someone if you say a friend or colleague of theirs suggested that you call.

You won't need to ask all of the questions suggested above. They are guidelines. Perhaps you can think of others which are of more interest to you. Remember how much you now know about your enjoyable skills and your interests, values and work satisfactions, and people and work preferences. Look again at your butterfly. Ask questions that will provide the information which you have indentified as important to you. For example, if you have decided that it is important for you to work as a part of a team with other people, perhaps you should ask if she knows other vets who work as part of a team. Don't forget to ask the information which you need to make intelligent and knowledgeable career decisions.

Within a few days after your interview, remember to send a "thank you" note. The person you interviewed has been generous with his or her time and taken an interest in your career planning. The note can be short, but the courtesy and appreciation will always be welcome.

The more people you speak with, the more referrals to others doing the same, or variations of the same, work. Perhaps you learned that veterinarian medicine requires graduate-school training, but you also learned that a veterinarian's assistant requires only two years of post-high-school training. With each interview, you will have a better idea of whether or not this career might be for you. So, you will not only be expanding your list, you will also be gathering information with which to narrow it as well. As you continue interviewing and get a clearer picture of a particular career, you will be better able to decide which careers to eliminate from your list.

Keep your eyes and ears open; ask questions. Provide opportunities for yourself to learn as much as you can about a career before persuing the needed experience and education. Know what you are getting into before you receive your first paycheck!

If you have come this far, *bravo*! I know the work has required a great deal of time and thought. My experience has been that everyone who has spent the time and effort evaluating who they are and what they want to be when they grow up has felt that the energy expended was well worth the resulting personal growth and career insights. I hope you feel the same way.

I, myself, will never stop asking the question, "Ellen, what *else* do you want to be when you grow up?" and I was 35 last March!

ঙ • ঙ

EDUCATIONAL AND CAREER DECISIONS, STRATEGIES AND GOALS

Sally Bemis is a nurse. She is also a graduate student in public health. She is an unusual woman. She is unusual because she has persistently set education and work goals for herself and methodically fulfilled them.

Young people who have career goals plan their college years, their work experience, their priorities at work and home, their moves, promotions, acceptance of one job over another, with an eye to whatever goals they set. As they achieve their goals, and as they change and learn more skills and see their own potential more clearly, they set new ones.

Young women are just beginning to learn more about career goals. Their goals usually end with marriage or a baby. They tend not to make decisions and plan a strategy for fulfilling a career goal at an age when they can do most about such a goal—in school or during the first years of a job. They credit luck for the good jobs they do get, rather than their qualifications or skills. They seldom plan to be in the right place at the right time for terrific jobs; if they happen to be, that also is "luck."

In an age when most mothers of young children work, and when that work earns no more than 60 cents

for every dollar earned by a man, it's high time that
women started planning their career goals, too. In an
age where a woman's median earnings are $8,600 com-
pared to $14,600 for men, it's high time for young
women to plan their strategies to get in on the money.
When you read about more and more women joining
the labor force, you may assume that they are entering
in all jobs and at all levels of work. What you don't
read is that the earnings gap between men and women
is worse than ever, in spite of the women's movement,
simply because women are still concentrated in the traditional, low-paying, female jobs. Six out of ten women
are employed in clerical, service, and retail jobs. And
on the professional level, women are almost all in nursing, teaching and social-service jobs.

 - If you are going to work (and most mothers do),
then wouldn't you like to be in on designing your
career, so that you will be working both where the
money is and at a job you would like to be doing? And
in a career that is meaningful to you? Of course you
would! Doesn't it make sense that if you have to work,
you'll want to work where you choose to be at a salary
that makes it all worth while? Men have known all
along what a few women are just beginning to learn—
that they can plan, organize, make decisions and set
career goals that they value.

When Sally Bemis was in high school, becoming a
nurse was her career goal. After achieving that goal,
after spending two years working in a hospital where
she learned more about her interests and values in
nursing, she set another goal. She decided to get a college degree in nursing, the necessary credential for a
supervisory job. She wanted the kind of administrative
work and responsibility that she saw her own supervi-
sors enjoying in the hospital.

Sally moved from the West Coast to a small mid-
western city, where she took a job in a teaching hospital and learned to see nursing in the wider range of
health work. As she learned more about the range of
job possibilities, she became interested in home health
care. She applied for a job as director of the Visiting
Nurses' Association—and was accepted.

After seven years on the job, marriage and two children, Sally realized that her next goal had to be for a job in the field of community and public health. Clearly seeing the necessity for more education to eventually get where she wanted to be, it was worth it to Sally to leave her job and family and go back to school for a year for a MPH (Master's in Public Health).

She was well established in her work before she made this decision. Because of her work experience and career achievements, she could arrange to take a leave of absence from the directorship of the VNA, to get half-pay while she was gone, and she and her husband had saved enough money to afford childcare while she was away.

Of all the outstanding things you can learn from Sally Bemis, the most helpful to you is her example of how a woman can set her own goals and plan the necessary strategy to go after them—even with a family.

Setting career goals is not only for women who end up in graduate school, it's also for those in business—and for teachers who want to be administrators, for engineers who want to direct a project and for reporters who want to get top assignments.

FEMALE EXPECTATIONS

The main reason you aren't into career goals more than you are is because you are not expected to be. A young woman who is interested in choosing a career is in a very different position from a young man. You are expected to be financially supported by someone else when you grow up. He is expected to financially support himself plus others when he grows up. You have been programmed to count most according to the money your husband makes. He has been programmed to measure himself as a person who counts most according to the money he makes. You are expected to find self-esteem through your family. He is expected to find his worth through his career. You have been programmed as a "sex object." He has been programmed as a "success object." The more you understand how you are systematically set up for certain choices, the more you will see a chance to vary that system.

Given that women are brought up differently and treated differently in both school and at work than men are, you have to accept these differences—and the anxiety that goes with them—before you can seriously plan your strategy for change. You may always be in conflict over achieving success in your career *and* being a successful mother. You may always be worried about personal criticism in your work in ways that don't bother your husband or male competition. You may always find it hard to be assertive and initiate your plans and your ideas compared to the ease your brother has with the same business behavior. In other words, women have to *learn* to manage *by accepting* the traditional conflicts of successful women. A woman must be able to say with confidence that she wants a career, and that she is willing to confront the conflicts that she will have *because* she is a woman. This advice is not only for women planning to go into business and management, it is also for women intending to go into law, politics, theology, engineering, medicine, mathematics, science, health administration and *wherever the men are*. For wherever the men are is where the money and policy-making is.

LOVE AND MONEY

One way that young women avoid setting career goals is by getting themselves into the false bind of choosing between love (marriage) and money (a good career). No one should have to make that choice! Instead of the love-or-money question, you should concentrate on where you want to be five years from now. Ten and 15 years from now. Do you want to be married? Do you want children, and when do you want to have them? Where do you want to be in your career development?

If you are like most women, you will end up marrying, having a baby *and* working. The fact that will be most helpful for you right now is that wanting to marry and raise a family doesn't in any way exempt you from the responsibility of decision-making about your career development while you are still in school.

CAREER DECISIONS

Career decisions start when you choose your school courses and majors and, with after-school and summer jobs, when you decide which job to take, how much education you need, and which job you will take. Everything you do, every skill you learn, every interest you develop, helps build possible career decisions. Career development is everything you do in your life. You are already in a developmental process—no matter what you do about it. Having babies and caring for them is a part of that process, and a place where you learn transferable skills—just like a paid job is.

If you are still a student in high school or college, all of your curriculum choices are career decisions. If you choose algebra or general math in the 9th grade, you are opening some doors and closing others, depending on your choice. If you take the 4th year of mathematics, you are keeping options open for many more career choices at a later time. Your college choice is a career decision. If you choose specialty training, the military, an apprenticeship, or motherhood, you are making a career decision. You can learn transferable skills in all of those places.

As a student, your responsibility to yourself is best fulfilled by learning as much as you can about your interests and abilities. Learn what you can do and how well you can do it. Learn also about your motivation, your ambitions, your dreams, your hopes and fears. Choosing which courses to take, and which school or program to enter after high school all build toward the choices you will eventually have.

CAREER DEVELOPMENT

Learning as much as you can about yourself is the first basic step in your career development. Ellen Wallach's "Life Career Skills" (page 172) will help you take your first step.

The second basic step consists of learning all you can about work, about your career possibilities.

Choosing your college major, choosing summer work opportunities, and taking a year off from school work (stopout) are educational pathways to your career goals—and the third basic step in career development. Choosing a work experience where you can test your classroom ideas is a significant factor in this third step.

WORK EXPERIENCE

Paid or unpaid work is a strategy to gain the practical experience you need toward your career goal. The skills you learn, the visibility you have on a job, the people who learn what you can do and your observation of the work system are the things that count most in a beginning work situation. When you take a menial job, it can become meaningful to you if you learn the system of your company, or profession or department, and notice what everyone else does. How do others relate to what you are doing? What are the links between production and sales, or sales and marketing? Between finance and planning? How has the company actually defined the jobs? Which staff areas provide the move in which directions to get to what jobs? Where does your boss' job lead? Do you like your boss' job?

After a few years on a job, a young woman asked herself if she would like her boss' job. When she realized that she hated his job, and the direction a promotion would take her, she quit. She started looking at her own career goals in terms of seeing the direction of promotion open to her, and if that was where *she* wanted to go. She is now an executive editor in a major New York publishing house—because she learned to set her own goals and to plan the strategy it took to get her there. In planning strategy, you can ask: Which line of work provides the basic experience that this company or institution demands? Can a reading specialist become a superintendent of schools? Can an LPN become a health administrator? Can an RN? How about an RN with a Master's in public health (MPH)? Do editors or marketing people get the executive positions in publishing?

If goal-setting for your career doesn't make sense to you for who you are, and where you want to be in life, and you can't find other women to serve as examples for you, talk to your brothers and boyfriends and uncles and father about career goal setting. Notice what they have in mind, and how they make their experience count, no matter what the experience. When you start working, notice how fast the men move from company to company. They don't get attached to a company, and feel a loyalty that prevents them from moving to other places in order to find new experiences and more meaningful work. Men don't feel indispensable the way women are taught to feel—and if they *are* indispensable, they expect the title and salary that shows their worth to the firm.

As you start out in the job market, money isn't nearly as important for long-range goals as a particular experience is. More important is to measure immediate income against potential future income, where the job leads, and what skills you can learn. For example, Lieutenant Governor Madeleine Kunin of Vermont spent $30,000 in campaign money for a $16,000 job. She knows very well that she can make more money in business, or in a great variety of places with her particular administrative skills, executive ability and leadership. Putting her career goals first, however, she chose to work hard to win the election because she knows that this is the job that will develop her skills, and also provide contacts that will lead her to the job she is after—Governor or U.S. Congresswoman. The point of your immediate career strategy is to broaden your experience and skills in learning new jobs, being confident that you can learn new jobs and having people see you in a great variety of job functions. Your eventual goals are advancement and greater responsibility leading to offers of increasingly complex jobs.

EVERYTHING COUNTS

Although they don't always seem to be related, every work and school experience leads to the directions in which you can go. When you begin to notice how everything about a job counts, then your present school or work activity will take on new meaning. When the beginning engineer understands her top opportunities, then the tedious job of drafting other engineers' plans can become meaningful. When the mother who is at home manages the domestic life of four people, including a toddler and an infant, and sees it as part of her career development in learning transferable skills, the motherhood can become even more meaningful.

Your purpose in career exploration and development is to help you determine all the directions in which you can go, and to learn transferable skills wherever you are.

A HUSBAND'S SUPPORT

As carefully as you plan your career strategy, you can't go far if you are married without your husband's support. Hennig and Jardim, authors of *The Managerial Woman*, found in their research with women who were in continuing education programs, that it was crucial for women to share their goals with the people who are closest to them. Women who didn't share the intensity of their goals to go back to school, for instance, were the ones who didn't make it. Their husbands didn't really have any idea how important career goals were to their wives. Consequently, the husbands didn't share in the work at home and with the children. They didn't approve of the changes as their wives left home for school or work.

Others in the family *have* to take more responsibility when the mother leaves home for school or work. Both husband and children have to know about the goals of the mother in order to realize how crucial it is to her, and give her their support. The ones who pulled it off were the ones who had their family's support because they were clear about their career goals, and they shared these goals.

Liz Oliver is the director of a youth project in a small city. She has always held responsible and demanding jobs. About her husband she says:

"My husband is completely supportive and in agreement with my career goals. He is really helpful in my work. You see, we have both talked about the idea that if we both work then neither of us will have to work sixty hours a week in order to live the way we choose to live. We aren't high-falutin' or anything like that, but we want to live comfortably with two kids."

The wives who have their husband's full support are the women who are clear about their career goals and priorities, and can express them at home. They are women who find life wonderful.

THE FOCUS IS YOU

Take your educational decisions seriously—as if your life depends on them. Because it does. It's true that women are programmed to get married and live happily ever after. But they don't hear often enough that meaningful work contributes to that happily-everafter. A well-paid career is a good beginning toward a happy life.

You can't know everything about the changing world of work, employment conditions and the everchanging social situations for women. But if you stick with assessing your own skills; getting in tune with your values and interests as they change; sharing your career goals with your partner, boyfriend or husband; and keeping your career options open for new directions—you can't go wrong.

ABOUT THE AUTHOR

JOYCE SLAYTON MITCHELL is an education consultant, former school counselor, and writer in the field of career education and decision-making. She received an A.B. degree from Denison University and an M.S. degree from the University of Bridgeport. She is the author of two books, *Free To Choose: Decision Making for Young Men*, and *Other Choices for Becoming a Woman*, as well as *I Can Be Anything: Careers and Colleges for Young Women*, published by the College Entrance Examination Board. She is a contributor to several magazines, including *Seventeen* and *Ms.* She lives in Wolcott, Vermont, with her husband and two children.

Congratulations—But...

What about all those questions and problems that arrive with a new addition to the family? Here are several invaluable books for any new or expectant mother. They are filled with helpful hints for raising healthy children in a happy home. Best of luck and may all your problems be little ones!

☐	13742	**BETTER HOMES AND GARDENS BABY BOOK**	$2.50
☐	14391	**UNDERSTANDING PREGNANCY AND CHILDBIRTH** by Sheldon H. Cherry, M.D.	$2.75
☐	14278	**PREGNANCY NOTEBOOK** by Marcia Morton	$2.25
☐	14409	**NINE MONTHS READING** by Robert E. Hall, M.D.	$2.50
☐	12640	**FEED ME! I'M YOURS** by Vicki Lansky	$2.25
☐	14399	**SIX PRACTICAL LESSONS FOR AN EASIER CHILDBIRTH** by Elisabeth Bing	$2.50
☐	13624	**NAME YOUR BABY** by Lareina Rule	$2.25
☐	14277	**YOUR BABY'S SEX: NOW YOU CAN CHOOSE** by Rorvik & Shettles, M.D.'s	$2.25
☐	13901	**THE FIRST TWELVE MONTHS OF LIFE** by Frank Caplan, ed	$2.95
☐	14407	**COMPLETE BOOK OF BREASTFEEDING** by M. Eiger, M.D. & S. Olds	$2.50
☐	13711	**IMMACULATE DECEPTION** by Suzanne Arms	$2.95
☐	13895	**PREPARING FOR PARENTHOOD** by Lee Salk	$2.75
☐	12497	**PREGNANCY: THE PSYCHOLOGICAL EXPERIENCE** by Arthur & Libby Colman	$2.25
☐	13699	**MAKING YOUR OWN BABY FOOD** by James Turner	$1.95
☐	13961	**MOVING THROUGH PREGNANCY** by Elisabeth Bing	$2.50
☐	01271	**MAKING LOVE DURING PREGNANCY** Bing & Colman	$6.95

Buy them at your local bookstore or use this handy coupon for ordering:

We Deliver!

And So Do These Bestsellers.

☐	13826	**THE RIGHT STUFF** by Tom Wolfe	$3.50
☐	13966	**LINDA GOODMAN'S SUN SIGNS**	$2.95
☐	13030	**SOPHIA: LIVING AND LOVING** by A. E. Hotchner	$2.75
☐	01223	**SOME MEN ARE MORE PERFECT THAN OTHERS** by Merle Shain	$3.95
☐	01203	**WHEN LOVERS ARE FRIENDS** by Merle Shain	$3.95
☐	13410	**I'M DANCING AS FAST AS I CAN** by Barbara Gordon	$2.75
☐	13889	**THE BOOK OF LISTS** by D. Wallechinsky, I. & A. Wallace	$2.95
☐	13111	**THE COMPLETE SCARSDALE MEDICAL DIET** by Herman Tarnover & S. Baker	$2.75
☐	14481	**THE ONLY INVESTMENT GUIDE YOU'LL EVER NEED** by Andrew Tobias	$2.75
☐	13721	**PASSAGES** by Gail Sheehy	$3.50
☐	13723	**1980 GUIDE TO COUPONS AND REFUNDS** by Martin Sloane	$2.95
☐	14379	**THE GREATEST MIRACLE IN THE WORLD** by Og Mandino	$2.25
☐	13859	**ALL CREATURES GREAT AND SMALL** by James Herriot	$2.95
☐	13406	**THE MEDUSA AND THE SNAIL** Lewis Thomas	$2.95
☐	12942	**JOAN CRAWFORD: A BIOGRAPHY** by Bob Thomas	$2.75
☐	14422	**THE PILL BOOK** by Dr. Gilbert Simon & Dr. Harold Silverman	$3.50
☐	01137	**THE PEOPLE'S ALMANAC #2** by D. Wallechinsky & I. Wallace	$9.95
☐	13300	**GUINNESS BOOK OF WORLD RECORDS—** 18th Ed. by McWhirter	$2.95

Buy them at your local bookstore or use this handy coupon for ordering:

THE FAMILY—TOGETHER AND APART

Choose from this potpourri of titles for the information you need on the many facets of family living.

☐	14211	**LOVE AND SEX IN PLAIN LANGUAGE** Eric W. Johnson	$1.95
☐	14486	**THE PLEASURE BOND** Masters & Johnson	$3.50
☐	14217	**DARE TO DISCIPLINE** J. Dobson	$2.50
☐	13164	**A PARENT'S GUIDE TO CHILDREN'S** **READING** Nancy Larrick	$2.50
☐	13258	**P.E.T. IN ACTION** Thomas Gordon with J. Gordon Sands	$2.75
☐	12632	**LOVE AND SEX AND GROWING UP** Johnson & Johnson	$1.75
☐	14232	**THE BOYS AND GIRLS BOOK ABOUT** **DIVORCE** Richard A. Gardner	$2.25
☐	14572	**HOW TO GET IT TOGETHER WHEN** **PARENTS ARE COMING APART** Richards & Willis	$1.95
☐	12821	**ANY WOMAN CAN** David Reuben, M.D.	$2.50
☐	13624	**NAME YOUR BABY** Lareina Rule	$2.25
☐	13773	**YOU AND YOUR WEDDING** Winnifred Gray	$2.50
☐	11365	**OF WOMAN BORN: Motherhood as** **Experience and Institution** Adrienne Rich	$2.95

Buy them at your local bookstore or use this handy coupon for ordering:

TEENAGERS FACE LIFE AND LOVE

Choose books filled with fun and adventure, discovery and disenchantment, failure and conquest, triumph and tragedy, life and love.

☐	13359	**THE LATE GREAT ME** Sandra Scoppettone	$1.95
☐	13691	**HOME BEFORE DARK** Sue Ellen Bridgers	$1.75
☐	13671	**ALL TOGETHER NOW** Sue Ellen Bridgers	$1.95
☐	12501	**PARDON ME, YOU'RE STEPPING ON MY EYEBALL!** Paul Zindel	$1.95
☐	11091	**A HOUSE FOR JONNIE O.** Blossom Elfman	$1.95
☐	14306	**ONE FAT SUMMER** Robert Lipsyte	$1.95
☐	13184	**I KNOW WHY THE CAGED BIRD SINGS** Maya Angelou	$2.25
☐	12650	**QUEEN OF HEARTS** Bill & Vera Cleaver	$1.75
☐	12741	**MY DARLING, MY HAMBURGER** Paul Zindel	$1.95
☐	13555	**HEY DOLLFACE** Deborah Hautzig	$1.75
☐	13897	**WHERE THE RED FERN GROWS** Wilson Rawls	$2.25
☐ ☐	11829	**CONFESSIONS OF A TEENAGE BABOON** Paul Zindel	$1.95
☐	11838	**OUT OF LOVE** Hilma Wolitzer	$1.50
☐	13352	**SOMETHING FOR JOEY** Richard E. Peck	$1.95
☐	14687	**SUMMER OF MY GERMAN SOLDIER** Bette Greene	$2.25
☐	13693	**WINNING** Robin Brancato	$1.95
☐	13628	**IT'S NOT THE END OF THE WORLD** Judy Blume	$1.95

Buy them at your local bookstore or use this handy coupon for ordering:

Bantam Book Catalog

Here's your up-to-the-minute listing of over 1,400 titles by your favorite authors.

This illustrated, large format catalog gives a description of each title. For your convenience, it is divided into categories in fiction and non-fiction—gothics, science fiction, westerns, mysteries, cookbooks, mysticism and occult, biographies, history, family living, health, psychology, art.

So don't delay—take advantage of this special opportunity to increase your reading pleasure.

Just send us your name and address and 50¢ (to help defray postage and handling costs).

BANTAM BOOKS, INC.
Dept. FC, 414 East Golf Road, Des Plaines, Ill. 60016

Mr./Mrs./Miss_____
                        (please print)
Address_____
City_____State_____Zip_____

Do you know someone who enjoys books? Just give us their names and addresses and we'll send them a catalog too!

_____
Mr./Mrs./Miss_____
Address_____
City_____State_____Zip_____

Mr./Mrs./Miss_____
Address_____
City_____State_____Zip_____